Christmas Curiosities

A Collection of Rare, Enlightening, and Unbelievable Christmas Facts for Curious Minds

Bruce Miller

Christmas Curiosities by Bruce Miller

Christmas Curiosities: A Collection of Rare, Enlightening, and Unbelievable Christmas Facts for Curious Minda, Copyright © 2024, Bruce Miller. All rights reserved. No part of this book may be reproduced or transmitted in any form or by any means, electronic or mechanical, including photocopying, recording, or by any information storage and retrieval system, without written permission from the author and publisher, except for brief quotations as would be used in a review.

Cover by King of Designer. Images are from Creative Commons except where indicated.

ISBN 9798343214987

Christmas Curiosities by Bruce Miller

Table of Contents

The Hidden Wonders of Christmas! 1

The Enchanting History of Mistletoe. 9

The Origins of Christmas Carols. 12

How did leaving cookies and milk for Santa start? 15

Creating Fun Family's Holiday Traditions 16

The Legend of the Christmas Spider 19

The origins of Santa living in the North Pole. 20

The Miracle M61ovie 21

Why did the Christmas tree go to the barber? 22

The World's Tallest Snowman is a Snow Woman. 23

World Record for the Longest Sled Chain. 26

Washington Irving's Role in Santa's Sleigh Ride. 29

"Jingle Bells" originated as a Thanksgiving Song. 30

The Origins of the Christmas Stocking Tradition. 31

World Record for most Christmas lights. 32

The Yule Lads -- Iceland's Thirteen Santas 33

Santa's New Look. 37

The Ghost of the Greyfriars Churchyard 37

The Legend of Santa Claus: A Journey Through Time 41

The Snowball Debate. 45

The Enigmatic Poinsettia. 45

Christmas party 47

The Christmas Pickle Tradition. 47

The First Artificial Christmas Tree 51

Santa's Special Postal Code: A Canadian Holiday Delight... 52

A neighbor helps out 53

Stages of Life at Christmas Time 54

Hilarious Christmas Capers 55

World's most popular Christmas song 59

Christmas Question for the family. 60

A great gift 60

Who is Santa's favorite singer? 62

KFC Christmas in Japan 62

A few facts about St. Nicholas 63

Fictional Christmas Mysteries for Fun and Imagination. 67

Popular Christmas Cookies. 70

The White House Christmas Tree Tradition. 72

10 suggestions for creative Christmas gifts. 74

The Wonderful Story Behind "It's a Wonderful Life" 76

The Tumbling Christmas Tree 79

The Krampus! 79

Christmas was banned. 81

The Christmas Eve Heist (England, 1950). 81

The Ghost of Christmas Past (England, 1930s). 82

The Snowball Showdown. 84

The Great Christmas Caper. A Poem 85

The Mismatched Pajama Party 89

La Befana. 90

Shopping 91

The iPad and the Christmas Tree… 92

The Annual Night of the Radishes 93

Who invented Candy Canes? 94

Tom Hanks and "The Polar Express." 95

Roller Christmas 96

The Gingerbread man goes to school.. 97

Dutch shoes.. 97

The Christmas Cookie Catastrophe 98

The Origins of the Term "Xmas 101

Iceland and the giant Yule Cat... 102

Eating Caterpillars?.. 103

History of Eggnog... 105

The Misplaced Ornament Game 108

The Chaotic Thompson Household 109

Atheist.. 111

Twas the Night Before Christmas... 111

Why do we celebrate Christmas in December? 112

The Story of Rudolf.. 113

Oddities at Christmas Time Around the World. 115

UK: The Pantomime Pandemonium 116

Canada: The Polar Bear Plunge Prank................................. 116

Rockefeller Center's Christmas Tree Tradition.................... 118

Memorable Celebrity Christmas Stories. 119

The Essence of Christmas 126

Did you know? 127

The Christmas Miracle of the Halifax Explosion 128

The Deeper Meaning of Christmas 131

Final thought 132

About the author. 134

We Want to Hear from You! 135

References 137

Christmas Curiosities by Bruce Miller

"It's been said many times that the more we know the more we can spread the magic of Christmas."

-- Anon.

The Hidden Wonders of Christmas! Welcome to
a journey of Christmas joy through enlightening, fascinating, and little-known festive facts.

The holiday spirit is infectious, from twinkling lights and decorated trees to the melodies of carols filling the air. While many of us are familiar with the more common traditions and stories, learning countless fascinating and little-known facts about Christmas adds layers of richness to this beloved holiday.

Let's embark on a journey to uncover some of these hidden gems, each shedding light on Christmas's multifaceted history and essence.

The Christmas Truce of 1914 on the Western Front. The Christmas Truce of 1914 was such a heartwarming moment amidst the tragedy of World War I. Along parts of the Western Front in December 1914, soldiers from both sides spontaneously stopped fighting and emerged peacefully from their trenches on Christmas Eve and Christmas Day to mingle in no man's land. There, they exchanged food, gifts, and good cheer with their supposed enemies in a beautiful show of holiday spirit and common humanity. [1]

The truce began when German troops placed candles in their trenches and sang Christmas carols, which the British troops responded to in kind by singing their own carols from across the way. Soon, men from both sides ventured out to meet in the empty space between the lines, where they found more similarities than differences.

Small gifts like food, tobacco, and souvenirs were shared as a sign of goodwill. Even activities like joint burials and prisoner swaps took place, all to respect the significance of the holiday. In some places, the ceasefire lasted into Boxing Day or beyond.

While commanders on both sides disapproved, hoping to keep the animosity and violence going, many ordinary soldiers seemed ready for a brief respite from the horrors of war. They took the opportunity to interact peacefully with men they saw as enemies but who, up close, appeared remarkably similar to themselves. Acts of human kindness, like one soldier cutting another's overgrown hair, showed our shared humanity can overcome even the deepest of conflicts, if only for a day.

Through song, food, gifts, and friendly conversation across the lines, these brave troops found light in the darkness and reminded us of all of peace on earth and goodwill toward men.

The Christmas Truce 1914

On that special Christmas day along the Western Front, enemies set aside their weapons and met between the trenches as friends. Brave soldiers from both Britain and Germany came together in the spirit of peace, exchanging gifts of food and greetings with smiles and laughter.

If only for a moment, men who once were opponents now stood companions, sharing in the joy and goodwill that transcends all boundaries on Earth's holiest of nights.

The Christmas Truce Memorial

A memorial was placed in Saint-Yves (Saint-Yvon – Ploegsteert; Comines-Warneton in Belgium) in 1999, to honor the beautiful act of goodwill that occurred there in 1914.

Brothers in khaki exchanged gifts of food and tobacco, played games together, and even had a joint burial ceremony for soldiers who lost their lives in the conflict. This simple memorial cross standing today reads, *"1914 – The Khaki Chums Christmas Truce – 1999 – 85 Years – Lest We Forget," helping all who pass by remember that even in the darkest of times, the light of our shared humanity can bring people together.*

The tradition of Christmas trees started in Germany, not Bethlehem. The first record of a decorated Christmas tree comes from Germany in the 16th century. Martin Luther is believed to have decorated a fir tree with candles to represent the stars in the night sky. In the 19th Century, the tradition of a Christmas tree began to spread from Germany to England and the United States.

Coca-Cola created Santa's red suit. Santa Claus was originally depicted wearing assorted colors, including green. But in 1931, Coca-Cola launched an ad campaign featuring Santa in a red coat, and the image stuck. The company's marketing department is largely credited with popularizing the image of Santa in the red and white suit we know today.

Here is how that happened. In 1931, The Coca-Cola Company commissioned American illustrator Haddon Sundblom to develop imagery of Santa Claus for use in the company's Christmas season advertising. Inspired by Clement Clarke Moore's 1823 poem 'Twas the Night Before Christmas", often known as "A Visit from St. Nicholas," Sundblom painted a version of Santa that diverged from traditional portrayals of the character. His interpretation depicted a round-faced, joyous Santa with a full, white beard and twinkling eyes, dressed in red garments trimmed with white fur.

This cheerful image of Santa became tremendously popular as it featured prominently in Coca-Cola's nationwide advertising for over thirty years. Sundblom's work helped to standardize the physical depiction of Santa that is so widely recognized today. Through a ubiquitous national advertising campaign, Coca-Cola played an instrumental role in shaping modern perceptions of Santa Claus as the warm, friendly symbol of Christmas that endures in popular culture. There is more about Haddon Sundblom later in this book.

"Jingle Bells" was the first song played in outer space. According to records kept by Guinness World Records, on December 16, 1965, the well-known Christmas tune "Jingle Bells" was broadcast during a mission undertaken by the National Aeronautics and Space Administration (NASA).

The transmission occurred as part of NASA's Gemini 6A spaceflight. Piloted by astronauts Wally Schirra and Thomas Stafford, Gemini 6A was conducting orbital operations when mission control radioed up to the crew, asking if they would like to hear a song.

Schirra gave his assent and mission control proceeded to pipe the festive lyrics and melody of "Jingle Bells" to the astronauts, who were listening in while circling the planet at an altitude of approximately 262 statute miles.

To date, this broadcast stands as the inaugural playing of a full song within the airless void of outer space, a milestone in the annals of space exploration, popular music, and the Christmas tradition.

The Fairy Tale Origin of the Gingerbread House Tradition. While gingerbread houses have their origins in the early 1600s, it was not until the publishing of the Brothers Grimm fairy tale "Hansel and Gretel" in 1812 that the tradition became truly widespread, particularly in Germany.

In the story, Hansel and Gretel come upon a witch's cottage in the woods that is constructed entirely from gingerbread, candy, and cake. Though grim in nature, this fairy tale helped popularize the idea of creating full-edible houses and structures from gingerbread and other confectioneries during the Christmas season.

In the centuries since, the tale has inspired generations of families across Europe and beyond to continue the tradition of baking and decorating their own magical gingerbread houses, keeping the story of Hansel and Gretel alive each holiday season through their colorful and delicious edible architectural creations.

Tracking Santa -- the wrong number turned into the right number. This is the story about the NORAD Santa Tracker: An Iconic Holiday Tradition Born From a Simple Misdial.

NORAD's primary roles include monitoring aircraft, missiles, space launches, and any airborne objects within or near North America on a 24/7/365 basis.

The tradition of tracking Santa Claus's global journey each Christmas Eve has brought joy to children and families around the world for over half a century. However, few may realize that this iconic holiday event originated from something as innocuous as a wrong number phone call placed many years ago.

In the mid-1950s, a young child seeking to speak with Santa Claus accidentally dialed the phone number for the Continental Air Defense Command's (CONAD) operations "hotline" in Colorado. Seeing an opportunity to keep the spirit of the season alive, the commander on duty that evening had his staff check the radar to pinpoint Santa's location. They then reported back to the child, step-by-step detailing his present whereabouts according to NORAD's military defense satellites.

Word of the lighthearted exchange quickly spread, and soon other children began phoning in each Christmas Eve hoping for a similar update on Santa's journey.

Since 1958, the North American Aerospace Defense Command (NORAD), which absorbed CONAD's roles and responsibilities, has proudly continued the tradition.

To this day, NORAD personnel devote their expertise to monitoring Father Christmas's flight across the globe, delighting children and families with real-time tracking updates through NORADSanta.org and associated social media channels.

A simple misdial truly became the small act that sparked a Christmas phenomenon still cherished by many after all these years.

Tracking Santa

The Enchanting History of Mistletoe. The twinkling lights, the scent of pine, and the sound of carols fill the air as the holiday season arrives. Among the many cherished customs that mark this joyful time, one stands out for its romantic and mysterious allure: kissing under the mistletoe. But where did this charming tradition come from, and why has it endured through the centuries?

The history of mistletoe as a symbol of love, fertility, and protection dates back to ancient times. The Druids, a class of Celtic priests, revered mistletoe for its supposed magical properties. Growing high in the branches of sacred oak trees, mistletoe was believed to possess healing powers, capable of warding off evil spirits and bringing good fortune. During the winter solstice, the Druids would harvest mistletoe with great ceremony, using a golden sickle to cut it from the tree and ensuring it never touched the ground.

The Norse mythology also played a significant role in the lore of mistletoe. According to legend, the god Balder, beloved by all, was prophesied to die. His mother, Frigg, the goddess of love, sought to protect him by extracting promises from all creatures and plants never to harm him. However, she overlooked the seemingly harmless mistletoe. The mischievous god Loki crafted an arrow from mistletoe, which ultimately led to Balder's death. In her grief, Frigg's tears transformed the mistletoe's berries to white, and she declared that mistletoe would never again be used as a weapon. Instead, it would become a symbol of love, and she decreed that anyone standing beneath it should receive a kiss.

The tradition of kissing under the mistletoe further evolved with the Romans. During Saturnalia, a festival honoring the god Saturn, Romans celebrated with feasting, gift-giving, and merrymaking. Mistletoe, associated with the goddess of love and marriage, Venus, was hung in doorways and used to decorate homes. It became customary for couples to kiss under the mistletoe as a symbol of fertility and a promise of future happiness.

The custom of kissing under the mistletoe gained widespread popularity during the Victorian era. The Victorians, known for their love of elaborate traditions and romantic gestures, embraced the mistletoe as a festive decoration. It was often hung in doorways and parlors, and it became a focal point for holiday gatherings.

The tradition held that a man could kiss any woman standing beneath the mistletoe, plucking a berry from the sprig with each kiss. When all the berries were gone, the kissing would cease. This playful custom added an element of excitement and flirtation to the holiday festivities, and it was immortalized in the literature and art of the time.

Today, the tradition of kissing under the mistletoe continues to be a beloved part of the holiday season. It evokes a sense of nostalgia and romance, reminding us of the enduring power of love and connection. Mistletoe is often used to decorate homes, offices, and public spaces, creating opportunities for spontaneous kisses and heartfelt moments.

The symbolism of mistletoe has also evolved to encompass themes of peace and goodwill. In times of conflict, mistletoe was hung as a sign of truce, and enemies would lay down their arms and embrace beneath it. This spirit of reconciliation and harmony is an important aspect of the holiday season, reminding us to cherish our relationships and seek unity.

There is science behind the magic. While the history and legends surrounding mistletoe are enchanting, the plant itself is equally fascinating. Mistletoe is a parasitic plant that grows on the branches of trees, drawing nutrients from its host. Its white berries and evergreen leaves make it a striking addition to winter decor.

Despite its parasitic nature, mistletoe plays a vital role in the ecosystem. It provides food and habitat for a variety of birds and insects, and its presence can indicate a healthy, diverse environment. The plant's ability to thrive in the harsh conditions of winter has long been seen as a symbol of resilience and life.

The tradition of kissing under the mistletoe is a testament to the rich tapestry of folklore, mythology, and cultural practices that have shaped our holiday celebrations. From the ancient Druids to the Victorians, mistletoe has been a symbol of love, fertility, and protection, bringing people together in joyous and romantic moments.

As we hang mistletoe in our homes and share kisses beneath its green leaves and white berries, we continue a tradition that transcends time and borders, celebrating the enduring magic of love and connection. So, this holiday season, as you find yourself standing under the mistletoe, embrace the moment and enjoy yourself.

The Origins of Christmas Carols.

Christmas carols have a long and varied history, originating from pagan songs sung at Winter Solstice celebrations. As Christianity spread, these songs were adapted to religious themes and became a staple of Christmas festivities.

One of the oldest and most beloved carols, "Silent Night," was composed in 1818 by Franz Xaver Gruber, with lyrics by Joseph Mohr in Austria. The carol gained international fame and was even sung simultaneously in English and German by troops during the Christmas Truce of WWI, symbolizing peace and unity.

Early Beginnings. The origins of Christmas carols can be traced back to pagan festivals held in Europe to mark the Winter Solstice. During these celebrations, people would sing and dance around stone circles, performing songs that were not specifically about Christmas but rather about the season and nature. These early carols were often celebrated in nature, meant to bring joy during the darkest time of the year.

With the spread of Christianity, these songs were adapted to reflect Christian themes. In 129 AD, a Roman bishop declared that a song called "Angel's Hymn" should be sung at a Christmas service in Rome. This marked one of the earliest instances of carols being associated specifically with Christmas.

During the Middle Ages, the tradition of singing carols became more widespread. St. Francis of Assisi is credited with popularizing Christmas songs in the 13th century through his Nativity Plays. These plays included songs or "canticles" that told the story of the birth of Jesus in a way that was accessible to the common people, using the local language rather than Latin.

The Evolution of Carols. By the 16th century, carols were more commonly sung in homes and on the streets rather than in churches. They were often performed by groups of "wassailers," who would go door to door singing and offering blessings in exchange for food and drink. This tradition laid the groundwork for the modern custom of caroling.

Many of the carols we know today have their origins in this period. For example, "The First Noel" and "God Rest Ye Merry, Gentlemen" are believed to have been written during the 16th or 17th centuries.

The Victorian Revival. Caroling experienced a revival during the Victorian era, thanks in part to figures like Charles Dickens, whose works emphasized the joy and goodwill of the Christmas season. The publication of "A Christmas Carol" in 1843, along with collections of carols, helped to popularize the practice once more.

Victorian society embraced caroling as a wholesome family activity, and many new carols were composed during this time, including "O Holy Night" and "Hark! The Herald Angels Sing."

Modern Day. Today, Christmas carols are an integral part of the holiday tradition, sung in churches, schools, and communities around the world. They range from traditional hymns that celebrate the religious aspects of the holiday to secular songs that capture the festive spirit of the season.

Caroling has also become a way to spread cheer and goodwill, with groups often visiting nursing homes, hospitals, and other places to bring joy through music. The tradition has traveled across cultures and countries, continually adapting and growing, yet always maintaining its core purpose: to bring people together in celebration and joy during the Christmas season.

In essence, the history of Christmas carols is a testament to the enduring power of music to unite people across time and place, celebrating both the sacred and the secular aspects of the holiday.

How did leaving cookies and milk for Santa start?
Why do we do this? Well, it started during the challenging times of the Great Depression. During this period of widespread financial hardship and economic struggle in the United States, parents sought ways to maintain their children's holiday spirit and sense of wonder.

Leaving a small gift of food and drink for the legendary gift-giver Santa Claus took hold as a means of reminding kids to retain their charitable nature, even in the face of their own family's challenges.

The milk and cookies were a symbolic offering to Santa from those who had little, expressing appreciation for any presents he might choose to leave in return.

Though initially borne of necessity, the custom endured long after the Depression's end as a means of fostering generosity, gratitude, and goodwill during Christmas – sentiments needed then and ever.

To this day, the milk and cookies remain a time-honored part of the Christmas Eve tradition in American homes, a small act with lasting meaning.

Creating Fun Family's Holiday Traditions.

Christmas has always been a time of joy, laughter, and a string of quirky traditions that have become legendary among friends and relatives. Although some of you may have heard of these, here are festive activities *with a twist* that you might not have considered to bring the family closer together and provide endless entertainment.

The Great Christmas Tree Hunt. The holiday season kicks off with the annual Christmas tree hunt. Rather than simply buying a tree from a lot, go into the countryside to select and cut their own. Armed with thermoses of hot cocoa and an old-fashioned saw, this is how one family sets off on their quest.

One particular year, the hunt took an unexpected and hilarious turn. After hours of searching for the perfect tree, they finally found one that met everyone's approval. As Dad began to saw the tree started to wobble. Suddenly, it toppled over, revealing a rather large and disgruntled raccoon that had been napping in its branches. Chaos ensued as the raccoon scurried away, and the family burst into laughter. Despite the initial scare, they managed to secure another tree and spent the rest of the day recounting the story, which has since become a family classic.

The Really Ugly Sweater Contest. Each family member is tasked with finding or creating the most outrageous sweater possible. It can get highly competitive and hilarious as everyone tries to become the Ugly Sweater champion! Remember color coordination may not be the right thing to do for this contest.

For example, one family member outdid herself by attaching battery-operated lights and a musical element to her sweater. As she walked into the living room, her sweater lit up and played a tinny rendition of "Jingle Bells," causing everyone to erupt in laughter.

Or dress up like a Christmas tree with lots of ornaments, mesh, fake snow, and tons of tinsel.

If you don't have an ugly sweater dress in different contrasting colors or dress all white, beige, or silver like a new fallen snow. Or dress up like a Christmas character like St. Nick himself, or Mrs. Claus, or Frosty, and mimic the mannerisms of the character. Most importantly, have fun!

The contest enhances a child's creativity and there is usually lots of laughs!

The Cookie Decorating Extravaganza. The kitchen becomes a hub of activity during an annual cookie decorating extravaganza. The family gathers around the kitchen table, armed with an assortment of cookies, icing, and decorations. While the goal is to create beautiful holiday treats, the event inevitably turns into a hilarious mess. For example, make a "superhero reindeer" cookie, complete with a cape and mask.

Or devote a competition to see who could make the silliest cookie, resulting in a table full of giggles and some unique creations. The cookies might not win any baking contests, but they're always a hit at the household.

The Secret Santa Swap. Most know the usual game of Secret Santa where gifts are anonymous and donors are revealed after the presents are opened. Here is another version of the usual Secret Santa gift exchange.

Names are drawn and everyone is to try and buy a **funny gift** under a certain dollar amount that has to reflect the recipient's personality or interests. The goal is to find the funniest, most unexpected gift possible.

For example, one family member might get a giant whoopee cushion from Secret Santa, or "dad joke" socks that play recorded puns when walking. For an adult, try a "wine glass sippy cup," for the avid wine drinker in the family. The Secret Santa swap always ensures a night of laughter and surprises.

The Christmas Karaoke Showdown. Have a Christmas karaoke showdown. Each family member selects a holiday song to perform, and the results are usually highly entertaining. Costumes, props, and over-the-top performances are encouraged, making for a night of unforgettable fun.

For example, two family members could do a duet of "Baby, It's Cold Outside," complete with a dramatic dance routine that will everyone in stitches. Or perhaps a family member might do an operatic version of "O Holy Night," hitting high notes that should leave the family both impressed and in hysterics.

The Annual Family Photo. However, this isn't your typical holiday portrait. Take the silliest, most outrageous photo the family can muster. For example, try having the family dressed as reindeer posed in front of a fireplace. Or, family members could dress as various Christmas movie or story characters, anything from elves to snowmen.

The Legend of the Christmas Spider.

The Ukrainians have a unique tradition regarding Christmas tree decorations, opting to use spiderwebs instead of traditional fairy lights.

According to an Eastern European folktale from Western Ukraine, the origin of tinsel on Christmas trees can be traced back to a small spider.

The story recounts how, one cold Christmas Eve, a spider who had just finished weaving her web for the winter was tired and hungry. As she rested in her web, she noticed a nearby Christmas tree that the local children had just finished decorating with cookies, garlands and candles in preparation for celebrating the holiday.

Intrigued by the twinkling lights and sweet smells emanating from the tree, the little spider climbed onto its boughs to get a closer look. However, the tree was so heavily laden with decorations that one of the top branches suddenly broke under the weight, toppling the tree over.

Just before it fell, the quick-thinking spider spun and flung her silken strands to catch the candles and secure the tree upright once more.

The children found the tree intact in the morning, held steady by the spider's web. They were so grateful that the decorations had been saved that they decided to leave the web on the tree as thanks to the heroic spider.

Over time, the shiny spider silk came to be known as "tinsel," and placing decorative spiders on Christmas trees became a holiday tradition as a nod to the Legend of the Christmas Spider.

The story helps explain the origin of these ornaments and explains why tinsel came to be a signature part of Christmas decor.

The origins of Santa living in the North Pole.

The traditional home of Father Christmas at the North Pole can be traced back to the illustrations of renowned political cartoonist Thomas Nast in the late 19th century. Prior to Nast's influential depictions, Santa Claus lacked an established geographical location. However, this was soon to change.

In the latter half of the 1800s, a spate of Arctic expeditions captured the public's imagination with tales of daring exploration in the far northern reaches. The North Pole in particular took on a mystique as an undiscovered territory at the top of the world. Nast strategically tapped into this sense of mystery and wonder with his artistic portrayals of Santa workshopping at the Pole.

Through his popularizations in Harper's Weekly, Nast cemented the North Pole as Santa's magical domain in the public consciousness. The timing aligned with burgeoning notions of the frigid Arctic as a land of fantasy separate from the everyday.

And so, Santa Claus found his home amid the ice and snow at the very spot epitomizing the unknown. Even today, over a century later, the images Nast conjured upkeep the spirit of Christmas rooted at the geographic North Pole.

The Miracle M61ovie.

When Natalie Wood starred in the 1947 film "Miracle on 34th Street," she was just eight years old but still held onto her childhood belief in Santa Claus. In her autobiography, Wood later recounted that during filming she genuinely believed the actor Edmund Gwenn, who played Santa in the movie, was Kris Kringle himself.

Mr. Gwenn would arrive on set incredibly early each morning and spend several hours meticulously wearing his costume and make-up applied, including a full white beard and mustache. Natalie said she rarely saw Mr. Gwen without his makeup.

At the end of production, there was a casting party where Natalie witnessed Mr. Gwenn without his Santa Claus attire for the first time. It was quite a shock to 8-year-old Natalie as she now understood and it took her some time to process it was just a role after all.

Besides his Oscar for "Miracle on 34th Street," he also won a Golden Globe and received another Academy Award nomination for the film "Mister 880."

.

Christmas Curiosities by Bruce Miller

Movie "Miracle on 34th Street

Edmund Gwenn

Why did the Christmas tree go to the barber?

A. Because it needed to spruce up before the big day!

Christmas Curiosities by Bruce Miller

The World's Tallest Snowman is a Snow Woman.

While most may assume the world's tallest snowman is a man, the fact is that the loftiest snow sculpture ever constructed was a snowwoman. [2] In 2008, residents of Bethel, Maine, and the surrounding communities spent one month building a snow figure that stood at an impressive 122 feet 1 inch in height and set a Guinness World Record. [3]

This unique snow creation is a colossal figure named Olympia the Snow Woman. The name Olympia was chosen to honor former US Senator Olympia Snowe from Maine (1995 – 2013). Constructed with approximately 13 million pounds of snow, Olympia was a marvel of winter engineering and creativity.

The Remarkable Features of Olympia. Olympia's design included several unique and imaginative elements that made her stand out:

- **Eyelashes**: Crafted from eight pairs of skis, Olympia's eyelashes were a whimsical touch that added a playful element to her towering appearance.

- **Hat**: She wore an enormous 48-foot-wide fleece hat, which kept her "head" warm and added a splash of color to the snowy landscape.

- **Nose**: Olympia's nose was an 8-foot-long creation made from chicken wire and painted cheesecloth, giving her a distinctive and cheerful look.

- **Lips**: Her lips were made from five red car tires, arranged to form a perfect smile that could be seen from everywhere.

- **Arms**: Olympia's arms were fashioned from two 30-foot-tall spruce trees, making her appear as if she was ready to give a giant hug to anyone who visited her.

- **Pendant**: She wore a 6-foot-6-inch-wide snowflake pendant, adding a touch of elegance and charm to her massive form.

- **Scarf**: A 130-foot-long scarf wrapped around Olympia's neck provided a cozy and vibrant accessory that stood out against the white snow.

- **Buttons**: Three 5-foot-wide truck tires served as buttons on her "coat," emphasizing her grand scale.

The Community Effort. Building Olympia was a massive community effort that involved the entire town of Bethel. Volunteers of all ages came together to shovel, shape, and construct the snowwoman. The project took over a month to complete and required the use of heavy machinery to lift and place the massive components.

Fun Facts About Olympia

- **Record-Breaking**: Olympia surpassed her predecessor, Angus, King of the Mountain, who was built in 1999 and stood at 113 feet 7 inches. Both records were set in Bethel, Maine, highlighting the town's dedication to creating monumental snow sculptures.

- **Visibility**: Olympia was so tall that she could be seen from miles away, attracting visitors from all over to witness this incredible feat of winter wonder.

- **Longevity**: Despite her massive size, Olympia stood tall for several months, gradually melting as the warmer weather approached. Her presence brought joy and excitement to the community throughout the winter season.

Olympia the Snow Woman remains a testament to the creativity, teamwork, and festive spirit of Bethel, Maine. This towering snowperson not only set a world record but also brought together a community in a celebration of winter's magic and the joy of creating something truly extraordinary.

If you want to see how Olympia the Snow Woman was created and all that went into building the snow sculpture, check out the YouTube video of Olympia's creation. It is referenced in endnote 6 at the back of this book. [4]

By the way, the world's tallest snowman is Angus, King of the Mountain built in Bethel, Maine then Gov. Angus King. The snowman was built in 1999 and stands about 9 feet less at 113 feet and 7 inches.

Christmas Curiosities by Bruce Miller

Olympia the Snow Woman in Bethel, Main [5]

World Record for the Longest Sled Chain.
Ever seen an extensive line of sleds? Do you know the Guinness World Record for the longest connected chain of sleds going down a hill?

In the picturesque village of Bramberg, Austria, nestled in the heart of the Oberpinzgauer region, a remarkable event was about to unfold. It was January 22, 2017, and the air was filled with excitement and anticipation as villagers and visitors gathered to witness a historic attempt to break a world record.

The Oberpinzgauer Fremdenverkehrsförderungs- und Bergbahnen AG had organized an ambitious challenge: to create the longest chain of sleds ever recorded.

The event was set against the breathtaking backdrop of the Kitzbühel Alps. Freshly fallen snow blanketed the landscape, and the sun shone brightly, casting a glittering sheen over the pristine slopes. The chosen slope for the attempt was a 600-meter stretch (almost a half mile long), renowned for its gentle incline and picturesque views. It was the perfect setting for what would become a momentous occasion.

Months of meticulous planning had gone into organizing the event. Volunteers worked tirelessly to ensure that everything was in place, from securing the sleds to coordinating the coordination of assembling the chain.

The Guinness World Records officials were present, ready to verify the attempt and ensure that all guidelines were met.

The participants came from all walks of life, united by a shared sense of adventure and community spirit. Families, friends, and even tourists joined in, eager to be part of the historic event.

The sleds, ranging from traditional wooden ones to modern plastic designs, were lined up in a seemingly endless row, each one tethered to the next with sturdy ropes.

Among the participants were local heroes and celebrities, including the mayor of Bramberg, who had enthusiastically supported the endeavor from the start.

Children giggled with excitement, while adults exchanged stories and laughter, the camaraderie palpable in the crisp mountain air.

As the start time approached, the atmosphere grew electric. Participants took their positions on their sleds, gloved hands gripping the ropes and eyes fixed on the slope ahead. The signal was given, and with a collective cheer, the chain of 508 sleds began its descent.

The sight was nothing short of spectacular! Like a colorful serpent, the chain of sleds snaked its way down the slope, weaving through the snow with graceful precision. The laughter and shouts of joy echoed through the mountains, a testament to the thrill and exhilaration of the ride.

The sleds moved in unison, each person relying on the one in front to maintain the chain's integrity. It was a true demonstration of teamwork and coordination, as any misstep could potentially break the chain and jeopardize the record attempt.

As the sleds reached the bottom of the slope, a roar of applause and cheers erupted from the crowd. The chain had remained intact, and the participants had successfully navigated the 600-meter descent. The Guinness World Records officials, clipboard in hand, confirmed what everyone had hoped for: a new world record had been set. The longest chain of sleds in history, consisting of 508 sleds, had traveled down the slope of Bramberg, Austria, in a stunning display of unity and determination! [6]

The participants, beaming with pride, embraced one another and celebrated their setting a World Record. The village of Bramberg had etched its name into the record books, and the event would be remembered for generations to come.

The record-breaking event brought more than just a moment of glory to the village of Bramberg. It fostered a sense of community and togetherness that resonated long after the snow had melted. The participants, from the youngest child to the oldest grandparent, cherished the memories of that magical day.

As the years go by, the story of that snowy January day will continue to be told, inspiring future generations to embrace the spirit of camaraderie and the thrill of achieving the extraordinary.

There is a video on YouTube of this amazing chain of sleds referenced in the endnote of this book. [7]

Washington Irving's Role in Santa's Sleigh Ride.

While Washington Irving is perhaps best known for his more gothic literary works like "Rip Van Winkle" and more notably, "The Legend of Sleepy Hollow" as that story instills a sense of dread in horror fans, he also played a key role in shaping our modern ideas around Santa Claus's transportation.

In his 1819 collection of short stories titled The Sketch Book of Geoffrey Crayon, Irving included a passage where he recounted a dream sequence that described Santa Claus flying across the night sky in a wagon pulled by reindeer. This fanciful description of Santa's ride through the air proved to be incredibly popular and helped fuel a Christmas fever that was spreading throughout America and England at the time.

Legend has it that Irving's festive stories served as inspiration for Charles Dickens' own classic Christmas tale A Christmas Carol.

While Washington Irving made his name in Gothic fiction, he also deserves credit for helping popularize the image of Santa Claus traversing the heavens each Christmas Eve in his famous flying sleigh pulled by reindeer.

Portrait of Washington Irving in about 1820 by Charles Leslie

"Jingle Bells" originated as a Thanksgiving Song.
While "Jingle Bells" is now synonymous with the Christmas holiday season, the origins of this well-known song can be traced back to a Thanksgiving celebration.

The song was composed by James Lord Pierpont and debuted in 1857 at a Thanksgiving program held at the Oneida

Community Church in Medford, Massachusetts where Pierpont served as organist. Pierpont wrote the lyrics for a Thanksgiving-themed performance to be accompanied by a church choir and organ.

However, over time "Jingle Bells" became disassociated with its intended Thanksgiving context. As winter weather provided natural imagery for a sleigh ride setting, the song took on new meaning linked to Christmas traditions of the period such as gift-giving, family gatherings, and festive community activities.

Today, "Jingle Bells" has endured as one of the most recognizable and beloved Christmas carols despite its origins lying outside the traditional Christmas song canon. The seasonal flexibility demonstrated in its history highlights how cultural context and interpretation can transform a work over generations.

The Origins of the Christmas Stocking Tradition.

The tradition of hanging stockings at Christmas can be traced back to the legend of Saint Nicholas. Known as a gift-giver to those in need, one story tells that Saint Nicholas wanted to help a poor man who lacked a dowry to marry off his unmarried daughters.

Seeking to provide the family aid discreetly under the cover of night, Saint Nicholas threw bags of gold down their chimney. The gold coins happened to land in the stockings the family had hung by the fireplace to dry. This act of generosity through an unusual method of gift-giving is credited with starting the custom.

Over time, Saint Nicholas became known as Sinterklaas to Dutch speakers. When his legend spread to English-speaking countries, he was eventually referred to as Santa Claus. To this day, the tradition of hanging stockings or putting out shoes on Christmas Eve is a nod to Saint Nicholas' original inspiring tale of using an unexpected route to deliver much-needed assistance to a family in need.

Families began hanging empty stockings or socks near the hearth on Christmas Eve, in anticipation that St. Nicholas might fill them with small gifts during the night. Gradually, children's stockings took the place of bags as the vehicle for receiving modest presents. Stockings offered an appealing Christmas symbol and a fun tradition for families.

By the early 20th century, the practice of decorating the fireplace mantle and hanging Christmas stockings filled with treats had become firmly entrenched in many Western Christian cultures. The origins of this festive custom can be traced back to that legendary act of kindness by the historic St. Nicholas so long ago.

World Record for most Christmas lights. The Gay family, residents of the Hudson Valley region, proudly

holds the Guinness World Record for most lights displayed on a residence. [8]

They earned this designation in 2014 when they strung 601,736 lights around their home in Lagrangeville!

Impressively, the family broke their own record the following year by setting up an even more dazzling display totaling 686,526 lights on their property!

The hundreds of thousands of lights installed in the family's yard are synchronized to play festive music while emitting a rainbow of changing colors. Visual highlights include illuminated reindeer and Christmas trees, sparkling stars, and trees adorned with colorful icicle lights twinkling in sequence.

Through technical proficiency and creative design, the Gay family has raised the bar for festive light shows and brought holiday cheer to their community on a grand scale.

Good Morning America did a YouTube showing of the house which is referenced in the end notes of this book. [9]

The Yule Lads -- Iceland's Thirteen Santas.

Christmas in Iceland is a season of enchanting folklore and delightful surprises, thanks to the presence of not one, but thirteen Santa Claus figures known as the "jólasveinar" or "Yule Lads."

These mischievous trolls each have their distinct personality and play a special role in the two weeks leading up to Christmas Day. The tradition is as unique as it is entertaining, filled with a blend of generosity and good-natured pranks.

The Yule Lads are not just ordinary gift-givers; they are deeply rooted in Icelandic folklore and their origins are intertwined with tales of mystery and intrigue. Each of these thirteen trolls descends from the mountains to visit Icelandic homes, one by one, starting on December 12th. They continue their visits each night until December 24th, spreading both cheer and a bit of mischief.

The Distinctive Personalities of the Yule Lads

Each Yule Lad has a quirky characteristic that defines their behavior:

Iceland's Yule Lads are a group of mischievous characters from Icelandic folklore who visit children during the 13 nights leading up to Christmas. Each Yule Lad has his own distinct personality and behavior. Here's a list with brief descriptions of each of the 13 Yule Lads:

1. *Stekkjarstaur* (Sheep-Cote Clod) – Known for harassing sheep, he has stiff legs, making his movements awkward.

2. *Giljagaur* (Gully Gawk) – He hides in gullies, waiting for an opportunity to sneak into the cow shed and steal milk.

3. *Stúfur* (Stubby) – The shortest of the Yule Lads, he is known for stealing pans to eat the crust left on them.

4. *Þvörusleikir* (Spoon-Licker) – Thin due to malnutrition, he steals and licks wooden spoons.

5. *Pottaskefill* (Pot-Scraper) – He snatches leftover food from pots.

6. *Askasleikir* (Bowl-Licker) – Hides under beds and waits for someone to put down their bowl (*askur*) so he can steal and lick it.

7. *Hurðaskellir* (Door-Slammer) – Known for his habit of slamming doors, particularly during the night, to disturb people's sleep.

8. *Skyrgámur* (Skyr-Gobbler) – Loves skyr (a type of Icelandic yogurt) and will eat all he can find.

9. *Bjúgnakrækir* (Sausage-Swiper) – Loves smoked sausages and hides and hunts for them then takes them.

10. *Gluggagægir* (Window-Peeper) – Peeps through windows to see what he can take from you.

11. *Gáttaþefur* (Doorway-Sniffer) – Has a huge nose and smells very well with it and uses his powerful sense of smell to find laufabrauð (leaf bread).

12. *Ketkrókur* (Meat-Hook) – This one uses a hook to take meat, especially smoked lamb meat. Uses a hook to steal meat, particularly smoked lamb.

13. *Kertasníkir* (Candle-Stealer) – Follows children around to take their candles made from tallow.

These Yule Lads begin their visits on December 12th, with one arriving each night until Christmas. They leave small gifts in the shoes of well-behaved children or terrible rotting and foul-smelling potatoes for those who have been naughty. Their mischievous antics add a unique and playful twist to Iceland's holiday traditions.

The Tradition of Yule Lad's Shoe-Gifting. During their thirteen-day escapade, each Yule Lad takes a turn visiting the homes of Icelandic children. The children leave one of their shoes in the window of their bedroom each night, eagerly anticipating what the visiting troll might leave behind. Good children are rewarded with small gifts such as candies, toys, or coins. However, those who have misbehaved may wake up to find a rotten potato in their shoe—a gentle but clear warning to improve their behavior.

Each morning, children rush to their windows to discover what surprise awaits them, fostering a sense of wonder and joy. The Yule Lads' nightly visits create a unique countdown to Christmas, making the holiday season in Iceland particularly memorable.

The Yule Lads were originally depicted as quite mischievous, even sinister figures, much like their ogre parents, Grýla and Leppalúði. Grýla, in particular, was a fearsome figure who was said to kidnap and eat naughty children. Over time, however, the portrayal of the Yule Lads has softened, transforming them into more benign and humorous characters who bring gifts and a bit of harmless mischief.

Today, the Yule Lads are celebrated as part of Iceland's rich cultural heritage, embodying the spirit of fun and generosity that defines the holiday season.

So, if you ever find yourself in Iceland during the holiday season, don't be surprised if you catch a glimpse of a troll peeking through a window. The Yule Lads are active, spreading joy and laughter, one shoe at a time!

Skyr the Yule Lad fond of skyr (sculpture at Keflavik International Airport)

Santa's New Look. Tired of his usual look, Santa decided to switch things up. He traded in his red suit for a sleek, green ensemble.

The elves were shocked, and Mrs. Claus giggled at his "fashion statement." However, the children loved the fresh look, thinking Santa had gone eco-friendly. By the end of Christmas, Santa learns that it's not about the clothes but the joy he brings. Yet, he kept the suit for St. Patrick's Day!

The Ghost of the Greyfriars Churchyard. In Edinburgh, Scotland, lies the ancient Greyfriars Churchyard, a site rich in history and lore. Known for its eerie atmosphere and storied past, the churchyard is often associated with tales of hauntings and ghostly apparitions. Among the most famous and well-documented is the story of the "Mackenzie Poltergeist," a spectral figure that has been witnessed by numerous people, especially during the Christmas season.

The History of Greyfriars Churchyard. Greyfriars Churchyard dates back to the late 16th century and is the final resting place for many notable figures, including George Mackenzie, a lawyer who earned the nickname "Bloody Mackenzie" for his role in persecuting the Covenanters, a group of Scottish Presbyterians. Mackenzie was buried in a mausoleum within the churchyard, which would later become the epicenter for paranormal activity.

The Initial Sighting. The first recorded sighting of the Mackenzie Poltergeist occurred on Christmas Eve in 1998. A homeless man, wanting some shelter from the Christmas wintry weather, broke into Mackenzie's mausoleum. Shortly after entering, he experienced a series of terrifying events. The man reported feeling an oppressive presence, followed by an unseen force that violently threw him around the crypt. He fled in terror, his story quickly spreading through the city.

The Christmas Eve Incident. The most famous and widely witnessed sighting of the Mackenzie Poltergeist occurred on Christmas Eve, 1999. A group of tourists, led by a local historian, had embarked on a ghost tour of Greyfriars Churchyard. As they approached the Black Mausoleum, where Mackenzie is interred, the air grew noticeably colder. The historian recounted the tale of Bluidy Mackenzie, and just as he finished, an eerie wail echoed through the churchyard.

The group watched in stunned silence as a ghostly figure materialized near the mausoleum. The apparition was described as a tall, shadowy form, cloaked in dark robes, with a gaunt and skeletal face. It floated above the ground as the group stood frightened with chills running down their spines. Some tourists reported feeling a sudden, intense pressure on their chests, while others claimed to have seen the figure's eyes glowing with an unnatural light.

The Aftermath. News of the Christmas Eve sighting spread rapidly, attracting paranormal investigators and curious onlookers to Greyfriars Churchyard. Over the following weeks, numerous people reported similar encounters with the Mackenzie Poltergeist. One family, visiting the churchyard on a snowy afternoon, claimed to have been chased by the spectral figure, which disappeared just as they reached the gates.

Local authorities took the reports seriously, and an investigation was launched. However, no logical explanation could be found for the sightings. The churchyard was thoroughly examined, but no evidence of tampering or human activity was discovered. The lack of physical evidence only fueled the legend, cementing the Mackenzie Poltergeist as one of the most compelling ghost stories in Scotland.

Subsequent Sightings. The Mackenzie Poltergeist did not limit its appearances to the Christmas season. In the years following the initial sightings, numerous people have reported encounters with the spectral figure. Tour guides, visitors, and even local residents have shared stories of feeling an unseen presence, being touched or pushed by invisible hands, and witnessing the ghostly form near the Black Mausoleum.

One particularly chilling account came from a security guard patrolling the churchyard late one night. As he approached the mausoleum, he noticed a figure standing in the shadows. When he called out, the figure turned towards him, revealing its skeletal face. The guard felt an overwhelming sense of dread and fled the scene, later recounting his experience to local authorities.

Scientific Investigations. The numerous sightings of the Mackenzie Poltergeist have attracted the attention of paranormal researchers and scientists. In 2000, a team of investigators from the Edinburgh Paranormal Society conducted a series of experiments in Greyfriars Churchyard. Using advanced equipment, they measured fluctuations in temperature, electromagnetic fields, and recorded audio and video evidence.

While the team did capture some unexplained phenomena, such as sudden drops in temperature and mysterious sounds, they were unable to definitively prove the existence of the Mackenzie Poltergeist. However, the sheer number of eyewitness accounts and the consistency of the descriptions lent credibility to the claims of a haunting.

The Legend Lives On. Today, Greyfriars Churchyard remains a popular destination for ghost tours and paranormal seekers. While some skeptics dismiss the sightings as mere folklore or psychological phenomena, the many people who have experienced the ghostly figure firsthand are convinced of its reality.

The Mackenzie Mausoleum in Greyfriars, Edinburgh, Scotland

The Legend of Santa Claus: A Journey Through Time.

The jolly figure of Santa Claus, with his red suit, white beard, and hearty "Ho, ho, ho!" is one of the most beloved symbols of Christmas. But the legend of Santa

Claus has evolved over centuries, shaped by various cultures, traditions, and stories. Let's embark on a journey through time to uncover the origins and development of this iconic figure.

The legend of Santa Claus can be traced back to St. Nicholas of Myra, a 4th-century bishop in what is now Türkiye. Known for his generosity and compassion, St. Nicholas was a beloved figure in his community. He was particularly known for his secret acts of kindness, such as leaving coins in the shoes of those who left them out for him.

One of the most famous stories about St. Nicholas involves a poor man with three daughters. Unable to afford dowries for them, the man feared they would be sold into servitude. Moved by their plight, Nicholas secretly delivered bags of gold to their home, ensuring the daughters could marry and avoid a life of hardship. This act of kindness cemented Nicholas's reputation as a protector and benefactor of the needy.

As the story of St. Nicholas spread, his feast day on December 6th became a time of celebration and gift-giving in many parts of Europe. In the Netherlands, St. Nicholas became known as Sinterklaas. Dutch children would leave their shoes out on the eve of St. Nicholas's feast day, hoping to find small gifts and treats left by Sinterklaas.

When Dutch settlers arrived in America in the 17th century, they brought their traditions with them, including the celebration of Sinterklaas. Over time, the name Sinterklaas evolved into Santa Claus, and the traditions associated with him began to merge with local customs and folklore.

The modern image of Santa Claus began to take shape in the early 19th century in the United States. In 1823, a poem titled "A Visit from St. Nicholas," more commonly known as "The

Night Before Christmas," was published anonymously. Later attributed to Clement Clarke Moore, the poem described Santa Claus as a "jolly old elf" who traveled in a sleigh pulled by reindeer, delivering gifts to children on Christmas Eve.

Moore's poem introduced many elements that are now central to the Santa Claus legend, including Santa's chimney descent, his sack of toys, and his ability to travel the world in a single night. The poem's popularity helped solidify these aspects of Santa's character in the public imagination.

The visual representation of Santa Claus was further shaped by the work of political cartoonist Thomas Nast. In the mid-19th century, Nast began creating illustrations of Santa Claus for Harper's Weekly magazine. Nast's drawings depicted Santa as a plump, cheerful figure dressed in a red suit trimmed with white fur. He also introduced the idea of Santa living at the North Pole and overseeing a workshop of toy-making elves.

Nast's illustrations played a crucial role in cementing the image of Santa Claus that we recognize today. His depiction of Santa's workshop and the North Pole added a magical, otherworldly dimension to the legend, captivating the imaginations of children and adults alike.

In the early 20th century, the image of Santa Claus received another boost from the world of advertising. The Coca-Cola Company launched a series of Christmas advertisements featuring Santa Claus in the 1930s. Artist Haddon Sundblom created the iconic images of Santa Claus for Coca-Cola, portraying him as a warm, friendly, and larger-than-life figure, always with a bottle of Coke in hand.

Artist Haddon Sundblom

Sundblom's illustrations were widely circulated and became synonymous with the holiday season. The cheerful, rotund Santa Claus in a red suit, as depicted in these ads, became the definitive image of Santa for generations to come.

While the American version of Santa Claus has become the most widely recognized, various cultures have their own interpretations and traditions related to the gift-bringer. In the United Kingdom, Father Christmas is a similar figure, though he has his roots in older pagan and Christian traditions. In Italy, children eagerly await the arrival of La Befana, a kindly witch who delivers gifts on Epiphany Eve.

In many countries, the figure of Santa Claus has been adapted to fit local customs and beliefs, reflecting the universal appeal of a benevolent figure who brings joy and gifts to children.

The Snowball Debate. It was a peaceful Christmas morning until the great snowball debate erupted in the North Pole. The elves argued whether snowballs should be round or square for the annual snow fort contest.

After much discussion, they decided to create a new shape—squound (square-round).

They found that if they tried to make the snowball perfectly round or square it took too long. If they packed the snow quickly in their hands, it would produce a mix of a squarish and roundish snowball or a squound snowball which could be packed and thrown quickly!

This compromise led to the most creative and fun snowball fight in North Pole history, proving that sometimes, blending ideas brings the best results!

The Enigmatic Poinsettia. The vibrant red poinsettia, synonymous with Christmas decor, has an intriguing history.

Native to Mexico, the plant was named after Joel Roberts Poinsett, the first U.S. Minister to Mexico, who introduced it to America in the 1820s. According to Mexican legend, a poor girl named Pepita had no gift to offer the Christ child at a Christmas Eve service.

Inspired by an angel, she gathered a bouquet of weeds, which miraculously transformed into brilliant red poinsettias. Thus, the poinsettia became a symbol of Christmas miracles and the beauty of humble offerings.

The Poinsettia is also widely viewed as a Christmas flower. Many gift the plant around the Christmas season to represent goodwill and community spirit. Within religious circles, some interpret the poinsettia's form as a symbol of the Star of Bethlehem, with its red leaves symbolizing the blood of Christ.

Poinsettia

Christmas party. At the office Christmas party, someone hung mistletoe in the most unexpected places—above the copy machine, the coffee pot, and even the exit door.

Colleagues found themselves in awkward yet hilarious situations, leading to laughter and friendly camaraderie. The mix-up sparked new friendships and reminded everyone that holiday cheer could blossom in the unlikeliest of places.

The Christmas Pickle Tradition. The Christmas pickle tradition was said to have its roots in Germany, brought to America by German immigrants in the 19th century.

While many believe this to be an old German tradition, known as "Weihnachtsgurke," evidence suggests that it might not actually be widespread in Germany at all. In fact, many Germans are unfamiliar with the concept.

Despite its murky origins, the Christmas pickle has become a cherished holiday custom for some families, adding a playful twist to Christmas morning festivities.

The custom involved hiding a pickle-shaped ornament deep within the branches of the Christmas tree.

On Christmas morning, the first child to find the pickle would receive an extra gift or a promise of good fortune for the coming year.

Though the origins of the tradition were murky, several delightful stories added to its allure. One legend told of a

Bavarian soldier named Hans, who was captured during the American Civil War. Starving and weak, he begged his captors for one last pickle before he died. Miraculously, the pickle gave him the strength to survive, and he later credited it with saving his life. Upon returning home, Hans began the tradition of hiding a pickle in the Christmas tree to bring good luck.

Another story suggested that the tradition was a clever marketing ploy by Woolworths in the late 19th century. The store imported glass ornaments from Germany, including pickle-shaped ones, and created the myth of the "German Christmas pickle" to boost sales.

In the Miller household, the Christmas pickle was the highlight of their holiday festivities. Every year, Mr. and Mrs. Miller would carefully hide the shiny green pickle ornament deep within the branches of their towering Christmas tree.

Their three children, Emma, Max, and Sophie, eagerly awaited the morning hunt, knowing that the finder of the pickle would receive a special gift and the honor of good luck for the year.

This year, the anticipation was even greater, as Grandma Miller had come to visit from Germany. She brought with her an authentic glass pickle ornament, intricately designed and shimmering with a golden hue. The children marveled at its beauty, adding an extra layer of excitement to the tradition.

On Christmas morning, the Miller children awoke early, their faces glowing with excitement. After a hearty breakfast of pancakes and hot cocoa, the family gathered around the tree. Grandma Miller, with a twinkle in her eye, recounted the tales of the Christmas pickle and the joy it brought to generations before them.

With a countdown from three, the children sprang into action, their eyes scanning the tree for any sign of the hidden pickle. Emma, the eldest, used her height to her advantage, peering into the higher branches. Max, with his keen eye for detail, examined every ornament carefully. Little Sophie, though small, was determined and methodical, checking the lower branches with precision.

As the minutes ticked by, the room was filled with laughter and friendly competition. Suddenly, a triumphant shout rang out. Sophie, her eyes wide with delight, had found the pickle tucked away near the trunk of the tree, hidden behind a cluster of sparkling lights.

The family erupted in cheers and applause as Sophie proudly held up the glass pickle ornament. Grandma Miller presented her with a beautifully wrapped gift, which turned out to be a handcrafted music box that played a traditional German Christmas carol. The room fell silent as the gentle melody filled the air, creating a magical moment that the Millers would cherish forever.

The discovery of the Christmas pickle brought more than just joy and excitement; it reinforced the importance of family and tradition. As the Millers gathered for their Christmas feast, they shared stories of past holidays and toasted to the memories they had created together.

Grandma Miller, with a tear in her eye, expressed her gratitude for being able to share this special tradition with her grandchildren. She spoke of the importance of preserving customs and passing them down through generations, ensuring that the magic of Christmas would continue to bring families together for years to come.

The Christmas pickle tradition, whether born from legend or clever marketing, had found a special place in the hearts of the Miller family and many others like them. It was a reminder that the true magic of Christmas lies not in the gifts or decorations, but in the love and togetherness of family.

As the Millers settled in for a cozy evening by the fire, they knew that the story of the Christmas pickle would be told and retold, creating a lasting legacy of joy and wonder. And so, the tradition lived on, bringing light and laughter to the holiday season, one pickle at a time.

A Christmas Pickle Ornament

The First Artificial Christmas Tree.

The origins of the artificial Christmas tree can be traced back to Germany in the late 19th century. At this point in time, there were growing concerns among the German population about the sustainability of harvesting large numbers of fresh-cut fir trees given the increasing demand to decorate homes and public spaces for the Christmas holiday.

To address the environmental impact of deforestation and develop an eco-friendlier alternative, early innovators had the idea to craft simulated trees using dyed goose feathers that could be reused year after year.

These feather trees, which were handcrafted by mounting the green-dyed plumage on wooden dowels or sticks, soon became a popular decorative option celebrated in German households. Not only did they help preserve the natural forests by reducing the need to cut down additional trees each season, but they also allowed families to display small Christmas ornaments in a similar manner compared to their living counterparts.

This novel invention combining tradition with environmental stewardship laid the foundation for the mass-produced artificial trees that have graced living rooms across the globe for generations since the 20th century.

What began as a German solution to deforestation concerns ultimately set the stage for modern artificial Christmas trees to become a widely embraced staple of the holiday season worldwide while still maintaining the spirit of the celebration.

Christmas Curiosities by Bruce Miller

Example of an Aluminum Artificial Christmas tree.

Santa's Special Postal Code: A Canadian Holiday Delight.

In the heartwarming world of Christmas traditions, Canada boasts a particularly delightful custom that brings joy to children everywhere: Santa Claus has his very own postal code!

Yes, you heard that right. The magical postal code "H0H 0H0" was created specifically for Santa within Canada's postal system. This clever combination mirrors the jolly "Ho, Ho, Ho" laugh that we all associate with Santa Claus, adding a touch of whimsy to the holiday season.

This is the story behind this unique postal code. Each year, the Canadian postal service is inundated with letters addressed to Santa or Father Christmas from excited children. To manage this festive flood of mail, they established the special H0H

0H0code, ensuring that every letter reaches the North Pole—or at least, its Canadian equivalent.

But the magic doesn't stop there. A resolute team of volunteers, lovingly referred to as "Santa's Elves," takes on the joyful task of responding to these letters. These elves work tirelessly, reading the countless heartfelt messages sent to "Santa Claus, H0H 0H0." Their mission? To ensure that each child receives a personalized reply from Santa himself, spreading holiday cheer and keeping the spirit of Christmas alive.

Imagine the excitement of a child receiving a letter back from the man in red, knowing that their wishes and dreams have been heard. Thanks to this unique postal code and the dedicated efforts of Santa's Elves, the tradition of writing to Santa Claus becomes even more magical.

So, next time you're helping a child write a Christmas letter, remember the special address: "Santa Claus, H0H 0H0." It's not just a postal code; it's a gateway to a world of wonder and joy, where the spirit of Christmas is alive and well in the hearts of children across Canada and beyond. Through this delightful tradition, the magic of Santa Claus continues to brighten the holiday season for all.

A neighbor helps out. During a neighborhood snowman-building contest, the Smith family's snowman mysteriously gained a hat, scarf, and buttons overnight.

The next day, they found a note from their elderly neighbor, Mrs. Parker, who couldn't join due to the cold. She wanted to participate in spirit and added her own touches.

Touched by the gesture, the Smiths invited Mrs. Parker for hot chocolate, showing that love and inclusion are the true spirit of Christmas.

Stages of Life at Christmas Time. In our lives, you first believe in Santa Claus with wonder in your soul. The first stage at Christmas time when you are a child is you leave out milk and cookies and wake up to find only crumbs remaining. You didn't know your parents were the ones eating the cookies!

The next stage is that you don't believe in Santa Claus anymore after you catch your dad "being" Santa on Christmas Eve. And you're so embarrassed that you believed for so long!

Many years pass and in the third stage, you find yourself dressing up as Santa Claus for the office, church, or neighborhood Christmas party and it's lots of fun and laughs!

Finally, after many, many years have passed, you look like Santa Claus! Between your red-cheeked belly laugh and full white beard, small children may stare with wonder at you as you walk by!

Hilarious Christmas Capers. Christmas is a time filled with joy, laughter, and sometimes, unexpected hilarity. Across the world, there have been numerous true and funny events that have added a special kind of cheer to the holiday season. Here are some of the most memorable and laugh-out-loud Christmas stories that have actually happened.

The Great Christmas Tree Caper (USA, 2008). In Portland, Oregon, the Christmas season of 2008 was marked by an incident that locals still chuckle about today. It all began when a family decided to surprise their neighbors with a grand gesture by placing a fully decorated Christmas tree on their front porch.

As the family sneaked across the yard in the dead of night, they carried the tree, ornaments, and lights, hoping to set it up without waking anyone. However, as they were halfway through their mission, the neighbor's automatic sprinkler system activated, drenching them and the tree. The family scrambled to turn off the sprinklers, but in their haste, they accidentally tripped the motion-sensor lights, illuminating the entire scene.

The neighbors woke up to the sight of their drenched friends wrestling with a soaked Christmas tree under bright lights.

Instead of being upset, they burst into laughter and invited the soggy culprits inside for a hot drink. The incident quickly became a neighborhood legend, and the tree, though a bit bedraggled, stood proudly on the porch for the rest of the season.

The Christmas Türkiye Escape (England, 2011). In Bristol, England, the Christmas of 2011 was unforgettable for the

Thompson family. On Christmas morning, Mrs. Thompson was preparing the turkey for their festive meal. As she opened the oven to baste the bird, their new puppy, Max, seized the opportunity and grabbed the turkey with his teeth, dragging it off the counter and through the house.

The family chased Max, who seemed to think it was a grand game, as he darted from room to room with the turkey in tow. The pursuit took them through the living room, over furniture, and even out into the garden, where Max finally dropped his prize in a pile of snow.

The turkey couldn't be saved, but the family couldn't help but laugh at the absurdity of the situation. They ended up having a vegetarian Christmas dinner, supplemented by whatever they could find in the pantry. Max, meanwhile, became the unwitting star of the holiday, and the story of the Christmas turkey escape is still recounted with laughter at every family gathering.

Santa's Stuck Chimney Fiasco (Canada, 2013). In Toronto, Ontario, the Christmas of 2013 was marked by an event that left an entire neighborhood in stitches. A local man named Dave decided to surprise his kids by dressing up as Santa Claus and delivering presents down the chimney. However, Dave had miscalculated the size of the chimney—and his own girth.

As he attempted to descend, he found himself hopelessly stuck halfway down. Unable to move up or down, Dave's muffled calls for help were heard by his family, who quickly realized what had happened. Someone called for help and firefighters rushed to the scene to rescue the jolly old elf.

The sight of firefighters pulling a laughing, red-suited Dave out of the chimney in front of a crowd of bemused neighbors was a scene straight out of a comedy movie. Dave's kids were initially worried but soon joined in the laughter, and the story of "Santa's Stuck Chimney Fiasco" became a local legend.

The Floating Christmas Tree (Australia, 2015). In Sydney, Australia, the Christmas of 2015 saw a unique and funny event that delighted beachgoers. A family decided to celebrate Christmas Day at Bondi Beach, bringing along a small, inflatable Christmas tree. They set it up on the sand, decorating it with lightweight ornaments and tinsel.

As the day progressed, a strong gust of wind caught the inflatable tree, sending it tumbling down the beach and into the surf. The tree, now bobbing in the waves, began to drift out to sea. Beachgoers watched in amusement as lifeguards launched a rescue operation, paddling out on surfboards to retrieve the runaway tree.

The lifeguards managed to bring the tree back to shore, and the family, though embarrassed, couldn't stop laughing.

By the way, the *Árvore do Rio* (Tree of Rio) holds the record as the largest floating Christmas Tree in the World according to the Guinness World Records.[10] It's in the heart of Rio de Janeiro, and is an extraordinary holiday tradition that lights up the Rodrigo de Freitas Lagoon each year.

It is an impressive 85 meters (278 feet 10 inches) in height and has become a symbol of festive joy and community spirit since its debut in Christmas 2007.

Sponsored by *Bradesco Seguros e Previdência*, the floating tree is a stunning feat of engineering and creativity. Adorned with 2.8 million micro lamps and wrapped in 37 kilometers (22.99 miles) of luminous hose, the tree radiates a mesmerizing glow that can be seen from miles away. Its dazzling lights reflect off the serene waters of the lagoon, creating a breathtaking visual display that enchants both locals and visitors alike.

Each year, the tree's lighting ceremony marks the beginning of the holiday season in Rio, drawing large crowds who gather to witness the magical moment. The floating Christmas tree not only illuminates the lagoon but also ignites the festive spirit, bringing joy and wonder to all who behold its brilliance.

The floating tree has become an iconic symbol of Christmas in Rio, celebrating the holiday with grandeur and adding a magical touch to the city's festive landscape.

The largest floating Christmas Tree, Rio de Janeiro

World's most popular Christmas song.

The iconic Christmas song "White Christmas" recorded by legendary American singer and actor Bing Crosby in 1942 has become a global commercial phenomenon.

Since its initial release over 75 years ago, the recording has reportedly sold more than 100 million units worldwide, establishing it as one of the best-selling singles of all time according to the Guinness World Records. [11]

Crosby's smooth baritone and the song's nostalgic lyrics struck a profound chord with listeners, tapping into universal sentiments of holiday warmth, family, and home. Since its debut, "White Christmas" has become synonymous with the Christmas season, featured in countless films and specials.

Over 75 years after its initial release, Crosby's signature version remains a staple of radio and holiday playlists each December.

Industry sources indicate that a sizable portion of the single record recording sales, estimated at 50 million or more, have come from the song being purchased individually as a single record rather than included within a full-length album.

This massive commercial success is especially notable considering "White Christmas" was released decades before the digital era we live in today, demonstrating the timeless and universal appeal of both the composition itself as well as Bing Crosby's beloved rendition that has become synonymous with the holiday season for generations of music lovers and Christmas enthusiasts around the globe.

Christmas Curiosities by Bruce Miller

Bing Crosby

Christmas Question for the family.

Q. How many "la's" are in the song "Deck the Hall?"
A. There are 96 "la's" in the song.

A great gift. Rudolph was feeling self-conscious about his bright red nose, so he decided to cover it with reindeer-friendly paint to blend in with his friends.

But during the Christmas Eve flight, the paint started to melt, and his nose shone brighter than ever.

Santa chuckled and reminded Rudolph that his unique glow was what made him special. Rudolph realized the love and acceptance from his friends was the greatest gift of all.

Christmas Curiosities by Bruce Miller

According to historical accounts, the iconic Christmas character Rudolph the Red-Nosed Reindeer nearly had a different name when first conceived by Robert L. May.

Specifically, Mr. May considered both Rollo and Reginald as potential names for the protagonists of his story before ultimately deciding upon Rudolph.

While Rollo and Reginald remain respectable names in their own right, Rudolph seems to have resonated more with audiences since its debut and become synonymous with the tale of the misfit reindeer who helps save Christmas.

The name Rudolph effectively captures the character's distinctive red nose and likely contributes to his enduring popularity across generations of readers during the Christmas season.

So, while the creator briefly weighed some alternatives, choosing Rudolph proved to be the right decision that allowed the story and character to make their mark on popular holiday tradition.

Christmas Curiosities by Bruce Miller

Rudolf the Red-Nosed Reindeer

Who is Santa's favorite singer?

A. Elf-is Presley

KFC Christmas in Japan. It has become a widely embraced practice in Japan to commemorate Christmas Day with a meal from Kentucky Fried Chicken (KFC). What originated as a promotional effort launched by KFC in the 1970s has since grown into a customary tradition for many Japanese individuals and families to enjoy the American fast food chain's signature fried chicken fare on December 25th.

Specifically, KFC leveraged clever marketing by tying their product to Christmas at a time when Japanese people were not familiar with the more typical Western traditions associated with the holiday, such as a turkey dinner. By positioning themselves as a unique option for celebrating Christmas, KFC was able to create a novel custom that resonated widely.

Now, decades later, eating KFC chicken on Christmas has taken hold as a common means of observing the holiday among the Japanese populace.

In recognition of the lasting tradition, KFC stores throughout Japan prepare extensively for the annual December 25th surge in business. Many customers even pre-order their holiday chickens weeks in advance to guarantee having their preferred pieces and quantities reserved and ready for pickup on Christmas Day.

The predictable high demand reflects how thoroughly engrained the practice of enjoying KFC for Christmas dinner has become in Japanese culture.

A few facts about St. Nicholas.

Saint Nicholas, known as the Bishop of Myra, was a revered Christian figure from the 4th century, born in the village of Patara in what now modern-day Türkiye is.

Renowned for his piety and generosity, Nicholas became the Bishop of Myra (now Demre) and was widely known for his acts of kindness, particularly towards children and the needy.

One of the most famous miracles attributed to St. Nicholas, the Bishop of Myra, is the story of how he saved three impoverished sisters from a life of despair. This tale not only highlights his generosity but also his deep compassion and resourcefulness in helping those in need.

In the town of Patara, where St. Nicholas was born, there lived a poor man with three daughters. In those times, a dowry was required for a young woman to be married, and without it, the daughters faced the grim prospect of being sold into servitude or worse. The man was heartbroken, unable to provide for his daughters' futures.

Hearing of their plight, St. Nicholas decided to help the family but wished to do so anonymously, in keeping with his humble nature. Under the cover of night, he secretly visited their home and tossed a bag of gold through an open window. This generous gift provided a dowry for the eldest daughter, who was soon married.

St. Nicholas repeated this act twice more, ensuring that each daughter had a dowry and could marry. On the third night, the father, eager to discover the identity of their mysterious benefactor, kept watch. When he saw St. Nicholas, he fell to his knees, overwhelmed with gratitude.

Nicholas urged the man not to reveal his identity, emphasizing the importance of giving in secret. This miracle of generosity not only transformed the lives of the three sisters but also became a cornerstone of St. Nicholas's legacy as a protector and benefactor, inspiring the tradition of secret gift-giving associated with his name and the modern-day figure of Santa Claus.

After his death, Nicholas was canonized as a saint, and his legend spread across Europe. He became the patron saint of children, sailors, and various other groups, celebrated on December 6th, St. Nicholas Day. His story was particularly popular in the Netherlands, where he was known as Sinterklaas.

The dowry for the three virgins (Gentile da Fabriano, c. 1425,)

The transformation of St. Nicholas into Santa Claus began when Dutch settlers brought the tradition of Sinterklaas to America in the 18th century. The name "Santa Claus" is derived from the Dutch "Sinterklaas."

In the 19th century, the image of Santa Claus began to take shape through literature and art. Washington Irving's writings and the 1823 poem "A Visit from St. Nicholas" (commonly known as "The Night Before Christmas") by Clement Clarke Moore portrayed Santa as a jolly, plump figure who traveled in a sleigh pulled by reindeer.

The modern image of Santa Claus was further solidified in the late 19th and early 20th centuries through the illustrations of Thomas Nast, a political cartoonist, and the Coca-Cola Company's holiday advertisements in the 1930s, which depicted Santa as the red-suited, white-bearded figure we recognize today.

Thus, the evolution of Santa Claus from St. Nicholas reflects a blend of historical legend, cultural tradition, and modern commercial influence, resulting in the beloved symbol of Christmas cheer and generosity known worldwide.

St. Nicholas, Bishop of Myra

Fictional Christmas Mysteries for Fun and Imagination.

In the quaint small town of let's call it, Frostville, Christmas was always a magical time. Snow would blanket the ground, lights twinkled from every house, and the aroma of freshly baked cookies filled the air.

Yet, beneath the festive cheer, Frostville was home to several unsolved Christmas mysteries that few people were aware of. These mysteries whispered about in hushed tones, added an air of intrigue and wonder to the holiday season.

The Disappearing Christmas Tree. The first mystery dates back to 1947 when the town's grand Christmas tree vanished without a trace.

Every year, Frostville's town square was graced by a towering evergreen, meticulously decorated with ornaments and lights. However, one frosty morning, the tree was simply gone. No footprints, no broken branches, nothing to suggest it had been moved. The townspeople were baffled. The local police conducted an exhaustive search, but the tree was never found.

Theories abounded. Some believed it was the work of pranksters, while others thought it might be a supernatural occurrence. Despite numerous attempts to solve the mystery, the disappearing Christmas tree remained an enigma.

The town erected a new tree the following year, but the 1947 tree's disappearance became the stuff of Frostville legend.

The Phantom Carolers. In the early 1960s, reports began to surface about a group of ghostly carolers who would serenade certain houses on Christmas Eve.

Residents described hearing beautiful, ethereal voices singing classic Christmas carols, but when they looked outside, no one was there. The phenomenon was always fleeting, lasting only a few minutes before the voices faded away.

Some residents speculated that it was a group of mischievous children, while others swore that the voices were too perfect to be human. Attempts to capture the carolers on tape or catch them in the act proved futile. The phantom carolers became a cherished, albeit mysterious, part of Frostville's Christmas lore.

The Snowman that Moved. In 1978, a peculiar incident involving a snowman was added to Frostville's list of Christmas mysteries. The Smith family built a large snowman in their front yard, complete with a carrot nose, coal eyes, and a top hat.

The next morning, the snowman moved several feet from its original position. The family initially thought it was a prank, but the snowman continued to move each night, always ending up in a different spot in the yard.

Neighbors watched in curiosity and tried to catch the snowman in action, but no one ever saw it move. Some suggested it was the work of frost elves, small mythical creatures said to inhabit the woods around Frostville.

Despite numerous theories, the mystery of the moving snowman was never solved. The Smiths eventually dismantled it, but the story lived on, captivating the imagination of the townspeople.

The Vanishing Gifts. In 1985, families across Frostville woke up on Christmas morning to find that some of their gifts had vanished. What made this incident particularly strange was that the missing gifts were always small but meaningful items: a grandmother's heirloom brooch, a child's favorite toy, and a father's cherished watch. The gifts were not valuable in terms of money, but they held significant sentimental value.

The town's police force launched an investigation, but there were no signs of forced entry, and the gifts were never recovered.

Some residents believed it was the work of a mischievous spirit, while others thought it might be a disgruntled townsperson. Despite the heartache it caused, the mystery of the vanishing gifts added another layer to Frostville's enigmatic Christmas tales.

The Unseen Benefactor. In the early 2000s, a new mystery emerged in Frostville. Each year, an anonymous benefactor would leave envelopes filled with money on the doorsteps of the town's neediest families. The envelopes always appeared on Christmas Eve, and the amounts varied, but they were always enough to make a significant difference for those struggling.

Despite numerous attempts to uncover the identity of the benefactor, no one ever succeeded. The benefactor's generosity became a cherished mystery, bringing joy and hope to the town.

Some speculated it was a wealthy former resident, while others believed it was the work of an angel. Regardless of the source, the unseen benefactor's acts of kindness became a beloved tradition in Frostville.

Create your own mysteries! The family could create their own holiday mysteries this year. Who took cookies from the cookie jar - was it Rudolph sneaking a snack or the costumed Grinch? As the scenarios thicken, remember that any missing presents under the tree will require one's own deducing rather than assistance.

By creating mysteries, one now must put on a deerstalker cap to solve the cases before ending up on the naughty list. Solving the mystery crimes could help spread some Christmas cheer and family fun.

Popular Christmas Cookies.

What do you think is the most popular Christmas cookie? The popularity of Christmas cookies can vary by country, region, and personal preference, but certain cookies have become iconic and widely beloved during the holiday season.

While there's no official record-keeping body that tracks the most popular Christmas cookies worldwide, several types of cookies are consistently mentioned as favorites in various surveys and articles.

Some of the Most Popular Christmas Cookies Include:

1. **Sugar Cookies**: Often decorated with festive icing and sprinkles, sugar cookies are a classic staple at Christmas parties and family gatherings. Their versatility and the fun of decorating them make them a favorite for many.

2. **Gingerbread Cookies**: Known for their warm spices and often shaped like gingerbread men or houses, these cookies are a holiday tradition in many households.

3. **Chocolate Chip Cookies**: A year-round favorite that also makes a strong showing during the holiday season. Some variations include festive additions like red and green M&Ms or white chocolate chips and cranberries.

4. **Peanut Butter Blossoms**: These cookies feature a peanut butter base and are topped with a Hershey's Kiss, making them a favorite for both their taste and their simplicity to make.

5. **Shortbread Cookies**: With their buttery flavor and crumbly texture, shortbread cookies are another popular choice. They can be plain or decorated with festive designs.

6. **Snickerdoodles**: These cinnamon-sugar-coated cookies are beloved for their soft texture and sweet, spicy flavor.

7. **Thumbprint Cookies**: Typically filled with jam or chocolate, these cookies are both visually appealing and delicious.

Cultural Variations. Diverse cultures also have their own traditional Christmas cookies that are popular within their communities. For instance:

- **Linzer Cookies** in Austria
- **Biscotti** in Italy
- **Lebkuchen** in Germany
- **Polvorones** in Spain

Surveys and Polls. Various media outlets and baking companies sometimes conduct surveys or polls to determine popular holiday cookies. For example, a survey by General Mills found that sugar cookies and gingerbread men were among the top favorites.

While there's no definitive record of the single most popular Christmas cookie, sugar cookies and gingerbread cookies often top the lists in various surveys and articles due to their festive appeal and widespread tradition.

The White House Christmas Tree Tradition. It has long been a cherished tradition for the President of the United States to display a brilliantly lit Christmas tree (also known as the Blue Room Christmas Tree) in the White House each holiday season. [12]

However, despite how firmly entrenched this practice is in American presidential tradition and custom, the precise origins and earliest adopter of the festive decoration remain unknown and unclear.

There exist two competing claims as to which commander-in-chief first placed a Christmas tree on display within the White House. Some historians argue that this honor belongs to President Franklin Pierce, who they allege inaugurated the tradition in 1856.

However, others contend that it was President Benjamin Harrison who introduced the Christmas tree to the White House in 1889.

While uncertainty persists around the very first incumbent to embrace this yuletide symbol, it is undisputed that President Calvin Coolidge established the formal White House Christmas tree lighting ceremony in 1923, a celebration that has endured as a national point of holiday observance for over a century since.

Thus, while the Christmas tree has long shone as a beacon of good cheer from the most famous address in America each December, the tree's precise origins within the White House walls themselves stay somewhat obscured amidst the mists of early presidential tradition.

In 1961, the then First Lady, Jacqueline Kennedy, started a new tradition of First Ladies selecting a theme for the White House tree. She chose them by taking the theme of Tchaikovsky's "Nutcracker Suite" ballet for the Blue-Room Christmas tree. [13]

Christmas Curiosities by Bruce Miller

President John F. Kennedy and First Lady Jacqueline Kennedy 1961.

10 suggestions for creative Christmas gifts. Here are a few creative and perhaps unusual gift ideas that will surprise and delight your friends and family at Christmas to bring a smile to their faces. These gifts and gifts like these can be found by simply searching online or you might find them in your local retail store close to you.

1. **Custom Bobblehead**: Have a custom bobblehead doll that looks just like the recipient.

2. **A subscription to an Exotic Food Club**: Set up monthly deliveries of unusual and exotic foods from around the world.

3. **Personalized Comic Book**: Turn a loved one into a superhero in their very own personalized comic book.

4. **Indoor Herb Garden Kit**: Allow someone to grow herbs indoors all year round, perfect for cooking enthusiasts.

5. **Levitating or Floating Bonsai Tree or plant**: A mesmerizing plant that appears to float in mid-air thanks to magnetic levitation technology.

6. **Virtual Reality Experience**: A VR headset or a gift card for virtual travel or gaming experiences.

7. **Personalized Face Socks**: Socks featuring the face of a pet, family member, or friend for a fun and individualized touch.

8. **DIY Hot Sauce Kit**: Everything needed to create custom hot sauces, perfect for spice lovers.

9. **Astronaut Ice Cream**: Freeze-dried ice cream as enjoyed by astronauts, a fun and space-themed treat.

10. **Miniature Zen Garden**: A tiny desktop garden for relaxation and stress relief.

The Wonderful Story Behind "It's a Wonderful Life"

Here's a heartwarming story about the making of a beloved Christmas film that might not be widely known. "It's a Wonderful Life," directed by Frank Capra and released in 1946, is now a quintessential Christmas classic.

The film tells the story of George Bailey, a man who, with the help of an angel named Clarence, discovers the profound impact his life has had on others.

While the film is now celebrated for its uplifting message and timeless appeal, its journey to becoming a holiday staple is both unique and heartwarming.

The Unlikely Beginning. The story begins with a simple Christmas card short story titled "The Greatest Gift," written by Philip Van Doren Stern. Finding no publishers interested, Stern printed 200 copies and sent them out as Christmas cards in 1943.

One of these cards found its way to RKO Pictures, which purchased the film rights. Eventually, it landed in the hands of director Frank Capra.

Capra immediately saw the potential for a beautiful, meaningful film and began adapting it into "It's a Wonderful Life." The movie was Capra's first after returning from World War II, and he poured his heart into creating a story that celebrated the value of every individual's life.

The Set That Felt Like Home. To bring the fictional town of Bedford Falls to life, RKO Pictures constructed one of the largest sets in film history at the time, covering four acres of the RKO Ranch in Encino, California. The set included a main street lined with 75 buildings, a tree-lined residential area, and even a working bank.

What made this set special was the sense of community it fostered among the cast and crew. James Stewart, who played George Bailey, and Donna Reed, portraying his wife Mary, often remarked on how the set felt like a real town, complete with neighbors and a shared sense of purpose. This camaraderie translated onto the screen, giving Bedford Falls its warm, lived-in feel.

The Impact of the Message. Despite its now-iconic status, "It's a Wonderful Life" was not initially a box-office success. It was only over time, particularly through television broadcasts starting in the 1970s, that audiences began to embrace the film's heartfelt message.

The movie's themes of hope, community, and the impact of one individual have provided comfort and inspiration to countless viewers.

A Real-Life Angel. A unique anecdote from the film's production involves Henry Travers, the actor who portrayed the bumbling but endearing angel Clarence. Travers had retired from acting before accepting the role, drawn back by the film's powerful message. His portrayal of Clarence, with his gentle wisdom and earnest desire to earn his wings, brought warmth and humor to the film.

Years later, Frank Capra shared that he received numerous letters from people who credited "It's a Wonderful Life" with preventing them from making tragic decisions, inspired by George Bailey's revelation of his life's worth. In a way, Clarence's mission to save George extended beyond the screen, touching real lives.

The Timelessness of "It's a Wonderful Life" Today, "It's a Wonderful Life" endures as a beloved holiday tradition, reminding viewers of the importance of kindness, community, and the profound impact each person has on the lives of others. The film's journey from a Christmas card story to a cherished cinematic treasure is a testament to the power of storytelling and the enduring spirit of the holiday season.

"It's a Wonderful Life"

The Tumbling Christmas Tree. The Smith family prided themselves on finding the largest Christmas tree each year. This time, they outdid themselves with a towering pine that barely fit inside their living room.

As they decorated, little Emily decided to climb the ladder to place the star on top. Just as she reached the peak, the tree began to wobble. In a flurry of tinsel and ornaments, the entire tree toppled over, covering everyone in a shower of pine needles. Instead of dismay, the family burst into laughter, untangling themselves and declaring it the best tree adventure yet.

They learned that sometimes, the best memories come from the unexpected moments.

The Krampus! In many European traditions, misbehaving children face more dire consequences than simply missing holiday gifts. In Austrian folklore, Saint Nicholas is accompanied by the fearsome Krampus on his visits to homes. Krampus is depicted as a horned, hairy beast who punishes naughty children in place of the gift-bearing Saint Nicholas. According to legend, Krampus will snatch disobedient children in his wicker basket and carry them away.

Many towns in Austria celebrate Krampusnacht on December 5th. During these celebrations, dozens of men dress in costumes depicting the half-goat, half-demon Krampus. They parade through the streets brandishing sticks meant to terrify any children who may have misbehaved that year.

While coal in the stocking is a mild threat in some traditions, the prospect of being snatched up by the monstrous Krampus surely gave European children added motivation to mind their behavior leading up to the Christmas season.

For most modern families, the fear of disappointing Santa Claus is deterrent enough without the need to involve such a creepy enforcer.

Saint Nicholas and Krampus visiting a child (1900s)

Christmas was banned. Throughout history, Christmas traditions and celebrations have been met with both support and opposition in various societies. In the mid-17th century, the English Parliament led by Puritans chose to ban Christmas festivities in favor of establishing a public day of fasting and prayer each December 25th.

The Puritans viewed Christmas traditions such as decorated trees, Nativity plays, and gift-giving as too lighthearted or frivolous compared to the religious significance of Christ's birth. This parliamentary ban on Christmas remained the official national policy in England from the 1640s through 1660.

The modern Christmas holiday was first legally established in the United States in the 1830s at the state level. Alabama became the initial state to officially declare December 25th a legal state holiday in 1836.

Over the following decades, other states gradually adopted similar recognitions of Christmas, with Oklahoma being the final state to do so in 1890.

While Christmas was not formally declared a United States federal holiday until 1870, its traditions had become widely celebrated across the country in the 19th century.

The Christmas Eve Heist (England, 1950). In 1950, a daring heist took place at the Brink's-Mat warehouse near Heathrow Airport in London. Thieves broke into the warehouse on Christmas Eve and made off with gold bullion, diamonds, and cash worth £2.6 million. The heist was meticulously planned, and the thieves managed to bypass the alarm systems and security measures.

Despite the high-profile nature of the crime and extensive investigations, the culprits were never caught, and the majority of the loot was never recovered.

The Brink's-Mat heist remains one of the most famous unsolved crimes in British history.

The Ghost of Christmas Past (England, 1930s).

In the 1930s, the quaint village of Alton in Hampshire, England, became the setting for one of the most enduring and mysterious tales of the era. As the Christmas season approached, the village was draped in festive decorations, with the scent of pine and mulled wine filling the air.

Yet, amidst the holiday cheer, an inexplicable phenomenon began to capture the attention and imaginations of Alton's residents.

It was a cold and crisp Christmas Eve in 1932 when the first sighting occurred. Mrs. Margaret Haversham, a local shopkeeper known for her no-nonsense demeanor, was closing up her small general store for the night. As she turned the key in the lock, she glanced up and saw a ghostly figure emerging from the fog that had settled over the village.

The figure was that of a woman dressed in Victorian clothing— a long, flowing dress, a bonnet, and a shawl draped over her shoulders. She carried a lantern that emitted a soft, ethereal glow, casting eerie shadows on the cobblestone streets. The woman seemed to be searching for something, her eyes scanning the ground and the windows of the nearby houses. Mrs. Haversham watched, frozen in place, as the figure drifted past her store and disappeared into the night.

Word of Mrs. Haversham's encounter spread quickly through the village. Initially, many dismissed it as a figment of her imagination or a trick of the light.

However, as Christmas Eve came and went, more residents began to report similar sightings. Each account bore striking similarities: a ghostly woman in Victorian attire, carrying a lantern, and appearing to search for something or someone.

The local children, both frightened and fascinated, began to refer to the apparition as "The Ghost of Christmas Past." They would huddle together, sharing stories and speculating about who she might have been and for what she was searching.

As the sightings continued, curiosity grew about the identity of the spectral woman. Some villagers delved into local history, searching for clues in old records and family stories. One name that frequently surfaced was that of Emily Chalmers, a young Victorian woman who had lived in Alton during the late 1800s.

Emily Chalmers was known to have been deeply in love with a man named Charles Whitmore, a local carpenter. According to village lore, Charles had promised to marry Emily, but fate intervened. On Christmas Eve of 1865, Charles was tragically killed in a freak accident while repairing the village church's bell tower. Devastated, Emily was said to have wandered the streets of Alton, searching for her lost love, until her own untimely death from a broken heart just a year later.

The villagers began to believe that the ghostly figure was Emily Chalmers, eternally searching for her beloved Charles. This theory seemed to fit the descriptions of the apparition and added a poignant layer to the mystery.

One Christmas Eve in 1938, a particularly chilling encounter took place that would forever cement the legend of The Ghost of Christmas Past. Reverend James Langley, the village vicar, decided to investigate the sightings for himself. Skeptical by nature, he was determined to either debunk the myth or uncover the truth.

As midnight approached, Reverend Langley set out with a lantern, walking the same streets where the ghost had been seen. The village was eerily quiet, the only sound being the crunch of snow beneath his boots. He reached the old oak tree where Mr. Blake had seen the apparition and waited.

Suddenly, a cold breeze swept through the air, and there she was—the ghostly figure of Emily Chalmers. Her lantern glowed with an otherworldly light, and her eyes, filled with sorrow and longing, met those of Reverend Langley. For a moment, time seemed to stand still. The vicar, feeling a deep sense of compassion, spoke softly, "Emily, if that is you, may you find peace this Christmas Eve."

To his astonishment, the ghost's expression softened, and she nodded ever so slightly. Then, as quickly as she had appeared, Emily Chalmers vanished into the night. Reverend Langley, though initially shaken, felt a sense of calm wash over him. He believed that his words had somehow reached the restless spirit.

The Snowball Showdown. During their annual Christmas gathering, the cousins challenged each other to a snowball fight. Teams were formed, forts were built, and the battle commenced. In the chaos, Aunt Linda, known for her peaceful nature, surprised everyone by launching a perfect snowball that landed right on Grandpa's hat.

The family erupted into laughter, and Grandpa playfully retaliated. The snowy fun reminded them that the playful spirit of Christmas knows no age, and the joy of family is the greatest gift.

The Great Christmas Caper. A Poem

It was Christmas Eve and all through the house,

Nothing was moving, not even a mouse.

But out in the yard, there arose a big clatter,

I sprang from my sleep to see what's the matter.

There stood my lawn flamingo, dressed as a deer,

With a red plastic nose and a hat full of cheer.

Next to him was my gnome, wearing Santa's own suit,

And a squirrel playing drums on an old Christmas boot.

Christmas Curiosities by Bruce Miller

The moon on the breast of the new fallen snow

Gave a cluster of noontime to objects below.

When what to my wondering eyes should appear,

But a miniature sleigh and some tiny reindeer.

But these reindeer were quirky, not your average lot,

They were juggling candy canes and doing the robot.

Dasher was breakdancing, Prancer played spoons,

Vixen told knock-knock jokes by the light of the moon.

On Prancer, on Comet, on Cupid, on Vixen,

They were knitting long scarves, each sporting a mitten.

Christmas Curiosities by Bruce Miller

Rudolph, the leader, had a disco-ball nose,

That lit up the yard in bright sparkly glows.

Santa emerged from the sleigh with a grin,

He was wearing a tutu and twirling within.

"Tonight's special, dear friends, let's dance and let's sing,

For Christmas is here, and it's a magical thing!"

So we danced in the snow, under starlit skies,

With reindeer and gnomes in joyful surprise.

The flamingo taught salsa, the gnome did the twist,

Even the squirrel joined in, it was pure Christmas bliss.

Christmas Curiosities by Bruce Miller

We sang carols with gusto, our voices so loud,

We drew quite the crowd, a spontaneous shroud.

Neighbors peeked out, then joined in the fun,

It was a Christmas Eve party for everyone.

When morning arrived and the sun started to peep,

The reindeer were napping in a festive heap.

Santa waved goodbye with a twirl and a cheer,

Promising to return the same time next year.

So if you hear a clatter out on your lawn,

Don't be alarmed, just put your slippers on.

It might be Santa and his oddball crew,

Ready to share Christmas magic with you!

    -- Anon.

The Mismatched Pajama Party. The Williams family had a tradition of wearing matching pajamas on Christmas Eve. This year, however, Uncle Joe was in charge of ordering them, and a mix-up resulted in a hilarious array of mismatched patterns and sizes.

The family couldn't stop laughing as they donned their eclectic ensembles, from polka dots to stripes and everything in between. They decided to make it a new tradition, reveling in the silliness and warmth that came from embracing imperfections and celebrating the uniqueness of their family.

These stories capture the essence of Christmas by highlighting the laughter, love, and togetherness that make the holiday season truly special.

La Befana. According to Italian folklore, La Befana flies down the chimney on her broomstick to visit each home on the Epiphany. So, on the eve of Epiphany, which falls on January 5th each year, families across Italy leave out a glass of wine and a plate of sausages for "La Befana."

The legend of La Befana originated from her interaction with the Three Wise Men who were following the star to witness the birth of Jesus Christ. When the Three Wise Men stopped to ask for directions, La Befana was invited to join them on their journey. However, she declined the invitation and said she was too busy with her housework.

After the Wise Men found Jesus, La Befana regretted missing the opportunity to see the newborn messiah. She then took her broomstick to fly around the skies of Italy each Epiphany eve, searching in vain for Jesus.

As part of the tradition, La Befana is believed to enter homes through the chimney and fill children's socks or shoes with candy and gifts for good boys and girls.

However, she also fills the footwear of naughty children with coal or onions. Her role on Epiphany eve helps reinforce the importance of good behavior as the holiday season ends and a new year begins.

The wine and sausages left out for La Befana are offered as thanks and sustenance for her travels on her annual mission to deliver presents across Italy.

La Befana

Shopping. The Friday and Saturday immediately preceding Christmas have become the peak shopping days of the year, rivaling even Black Friday in terms of traffic.

According to recent statistical studies, the ten highest-volume retail days in the United States now account for nearly 50% of all holiday shopping transactions, with the weekend before Christmas Day ranking amongst the top.

As for the entire winter sales season, the US National Retail Federation estimates total sales reached approximately $964.4 billion in 2023. [14]

This trend demonstrates consumers increasingly concentrating their gift purchases closer to the holiday itself. With two full weekends of shopping remaining before December 25th, retailers can anticipate record store traffic as families finalize preparations to celebrate Christmas.

The iPad and the Christmas Tree...

Q. What do you get if you cross an iPad with a Christmas tree?

A. A pineapple!

Q. What is a Christmas tree's favorite ornament?

A. An Orna-mint!

The Annual Night of the Radishes.

This event is a celebration held in Oaxaca City, Mexico and it's a long-standing tradition that draws thousands of visitors each year in the days leading up to Christmas.

While one might assume based on the name that it is referring to a low-budget horror film from the 1980s, the Night of the Radishes is in fact a competition focused on creative carvings crafted entirely from radishes.

Participants demonstrate truly remarkable artistry as they meticulously cut intricate designs ranging from classic nativity scenes depicting the birth of Christ to fantastical monsters and creatures straight out of imagination. For the duration of the event, the town's central square is transformed as display tables overflowing with the vegetable sculptures.

The radishes used in these carvings are specially cultivated to achieve immense sizes through strategic growing techniques and applications of agricultural chemicals. While pumping the radishes in such a way allows them to serve as viable materials for the carvers, it is a fleeting art form as the fragile nature of the raw sculptures means they only remain intact for a few hours before the effects of exposure cause them to quickly wither.

As such, the Night of the Radishes presents a unique temporary exhibition that draws widespread attention each year, if only for a brief window to admire the talent and creativity of the radish artists in Oaxaca City.

Christmas Curiosities by Bruce Miller

Radishes on display

Who invented Candy Canes?

Candy canes have become a beloved Christmas symbol and tradition in many homes across the United States. However, few may realize that candy canes have a long history dating back over 350 years.

According to records and research, candy canes find their origins in Germany in 1670. [15] It happened in Cologne, Germany. The choirmaster at Cologne Cathedral sought a way to keep the child members of the church choir occupied and silent during the tradition of the Living Creche on Christmas Eve. As such, he distributed to the children thin sticks of white sugar candy that were bent into a shepherd's crook shape. This innovative treat helped distract the young singers as they silently watched the nativity scene. [16]

Over time, the white candy canes were decorated with red stripes representing the hot pepper flavoring or the blood of Christ. Regardless of the exact symbolism, the distinctive peppermint-flavored hard candy has become a cherished part of Christmas celebrations around the world and remains a nostalgic favorite for both children and adults during the holiday season.

Tom Hanks and "The Polar Express." Beyond lending his voice to the mysterious train conductor who guides a group of passengers on Christmas Eve, Hanks inhabited a variety of other roles integral to conveying the story's key themes and message.

In addition to bringing the conductor to life both verbally and physically through motion capture technology, Hanks filled the shoes - quite literally in some cases - of several other parts.

Among these were the unnamed main protagonist referred to as Hero Boy, the boy's understanding yet concerned father, a lonely hobo the children encounter, Ebenezer Scrooge from A Christmas Carol, and of course Santa Claus himself.

Hanks' ability to inhabit such a wide range of characters, each with their own unique personality, mannerisms, and role to play in the narrative, was a testament to his talents and helped immerse the audience in the film's whimsical and heartwarming Christmas adventure.

Illustration from "Polar Express"

Roller Christmas. In the capital city of Caracas, Venezuela, large groups of urban residents utilize roller skates to safely travel to Christmas morning mass each year.

This tradition has become firmly cemented such that many of the city's roadways are closed to vehicular traffic beginning at 8 am, allowing the rolling congregation to reach their places of worship without concern for navigating motor vehicles.

Even the youth are said to participate in preparations for the festive event the evening prior. Tales indicate children will sleep with one skate lace tied around their toe and the companion skate dangling from an open window, permitting peers to gently rouse them from slumber through a cordial tug on the bound shoelace come dawn.

The engaged ritual reflects the deep-rooted nature of this unusual yet uplifting custom in the community.

The Gingerbread man goes to school.

Q. Why did the gingerbread man go to school?

A. He wanted to be a smart cookie!

Dutch shoes. Each December in the days preceding the 25th, Dutch youths anticipate placing their footwear by the hearth anxiously, hoping the famed Sinterklaas will generously stock them with modest presents and confections under cover of night.

In accordance with longstanding tradition, carrots are customarily left alongside the shoes as an offering for Sinterklaas' loyal steed, a white stallion called Amerigo.

In times past, misbehaving minors risked receiving a potato in place of gifts as a cautionary consequence for misdeeds, yet distributing potatoes in this punitive fashion is no longer deemed an appropriate method for discouraging untoward conduct.

While the exact origins remain obscure, this festive Dutch tradition continues delighting children each Yuletide with its lighthearted blend of fantasy and folklore.

Sinterklaas

The Christmas Cookie Catastrophe. It was the week before Christmas, and the Johnson family was knee-deep in holiday preparations. The house was decked out in twinkling lights, and the smell of pine filled the air. Carol, the matriarch of the Johnson clan, had a grand plan to bake the most impressive batch of Christmas cookies the neighborhood had ever seen. She had spent weeks gathering exotic ingredients and little-known recipes, determined to create a cookie masterpiece.

Then a large package arrived at the Johnsons' doorstep. It was from Carol's eccentric Aunt Edith, renowned in the family for her unconventional holiday gifts. Carol opened the box to find a strange assortment of cookie cutters shaped like kangaroos,

UFOs, and even a miniature Eiffel Tower. Alongside cutters was a note: "Use these for a truly unforgettal Christmas. P.S. Don't ask why."

Carol shrugged and decided to incorporate the odd shapes int(her cookie extravaganza. She gathered her family in the kitchen for a baking session.

Her husband, Bob, and their teenage kids, Jake and Sophie, were more interested in sampling the dough than helping, but Carol had ways to motivate them. "Anyone who helps gets extra cookies," she declared, and suddenly, everyone was on board.

Several pans laid on the counter for baking. Just then, the doorbell rang. It was Carol's neighbor, Mrs. Jenkins, who had come to borrow a cup of sugar. The Johnsons were fond of Mrs. Jenkins, mostly because she had a knack for getting involved in their most chaotic moments. "Oh my, what are you all up to?" she asked, eyeing the Eiffel Tower cookies.

They had just pulled the first batch of cookies out of the oven when disaster struck. The UFO-shaped cookies had expanded into unrecognizable blobs, and the kangaroo cookies looked more like squished frogs. The Eiffel Tower cookies had collapsed into piles of crumbs.

In an attempt to salvage the situation, Bob suggested they take a break and enjoy some eggnog. Carol had prepared a special batch using Aunt Edith's secret recipe, which included a generous amount of rum. Before long, the eggnog had everyone in fits of giggles.

Christmas Curiosities by Bruce Miller

Mrs. Jenkins tried to tell another Christmas fact but could barely get the words out. "Did you know... that... 'Xmas' comes from the Greek letter 'Chi,' which stands for Christ?"

Jake, inspired by the eggnog-induced hilarity, decided to create a new batch of cookies using his own "secret ingredient"—a spoonful of spicy sauce. He shaped the dough into tiny reindeer and popped it into the oven.

When the timer went off, the family gathered around to see the results. The reindeer cookies looked perfect, but as soon as they bit into them, their faces turned bright red. "Jake! What did you put in these?" Carol exclaimed, tears streaming down her face from the spiciness.

Amid the chaos, the doorbell rang again. This time, it was the entire neighborhood, ready for the cookie swap. Carol, Bob, Jake, Sophie, and Mrs. Jenkins looked at each other, then at the table full of bizarrely shaped, spicy, and crumbly cookies.

In a moment of sheer holiday magic, the neighbors loved the cookies. They found the odd shapes charming, the spicy reindeer adventurous, and the collapsed Eiffel Towers hilarious. "This is the most memorable cookie swap ever!" someone exclaimed.

As the evening wound down, the Johnsons, slightly tipsy from eggnog and high on laughter, realized that sometimes the best Christmas memories come from the most unexpected moments. Carol raised her glass and toasted, "To Aunt Edith and her crazy cookie cutters. Merry Christmas, everyone!"

And so, the Johnson family's Christmas cookie catastrophe turned into a beloved holiday tradition, filled with laughter, love, and a touch of chaos.

Christmas Cookies

The Origins of the Term "Xmas. "Xmas" is sometimes viewed as a recent secular abbreviation for Christmas, the term actually dates back several centuries. The word Xmas finds its roots in the Greek letter Chi, which is represented by the English letter X. [17] As Mrs. Jenkins said in the previous story, Chi was one of the early abbreviations used to represent Christ's name, as it is the first letter of "Christ" in Greek, which is *Χριστός*.

By the mid-1500s, the letter X had become a common abbreviation for Christ or Christmas when writing in the Greek tradition. This was adapted in some texts written in Latin as well. Over time, this Greek-derived X came to be used as a shorthand way to reference the celebration of Christmas in certain texts and writings in English.

Therefore, while it may seem a modern shorthand, the use of "Xmas" to refer to Christmas has historical precedence dating back to the 16th century and the early use of X as an abbreviation for Christ or his name in some language and spiritual traditions.

Iceland and the giant Yule Cat.

One of the more unique festive traditions that has been documented originates from Iceland. Folklore from the region describes a giant cat said to roam the snow-covered countryside during the Christmas season.

By tradition, farmers would employ the menacing Yule Cat, as incentive for their workers and laborers to be diligent in their tasks - those who demonstrated a strong work ethic through the holidays would be rewarded with a new set of warm clothing, while any shirkers or slackers risked facing a most ghastly fate of being devoured by the formidable feline beast.

This giant cat is called Jólakötturinn and the legend tells of Jólakötturinn attacking and eating people who did not have new clothes at Christmas time. [18] The Yule Cat is the house pet of Yule Lad Gryla.

This legend was often told to children in order to motivate them to finish their chores and duties in a timely manner in the weeks leading up to Christmas.

In modern times in Iceland, it has become a customary practice for all residents of the nation to receive new apparel during the Yuletide holidays. This tradition is thought to serve as a continued tribute to the old tales and also helps ensure no one has to endure the dreadful demise supposedly threatened by the

History of Eggnog. The precise origins of the name "eggnog" have been debated by linguists and historians for some time. While no definitive evidence exists, the prevailing theories point to two key elements that likely combined to form this festive winter beverage's moniker.

Firstly, eggs are a signature ingredient in traditional eggnog recipes, providing the drink's characteristic rich, creamy texture through the use of beaten egg yolks or whole eggs. The inclusion of this protein-rich foodstuff directly connects to the first half of the name.

The latter component, "nog," has several potential etymological roots that scholars have proposed over the years. One idea is that it derives from the word "noggin," a small cup or mug that was commonly used to serve ale or other alcoholic drinks in medieval Europe.

Another theory puts forth that "nog" refers to a type of strong ale or variety of beer consumed in England during the same period.

Regardless of the precise linguistic origins, we know that eggnog finds its cultural beginnings in the culinary traditions of Britain centuries ago. Medieval cooks developed early formulations utilizing milk and eggs, ingredients native to their region, with alcohol sometimes added to yield a revitalizing beverage. Through the passing of time and cultural exchange, this prototype evolved into today's familiar spiced, sweetened eggnog so enjoyed during the Christmas holiday season in many parts of the world.

While questions remain around specifics of its name, eggnog's history and appeal have endured. During the 18th century, rum imported from the Caribbean islands was commonly used as the primary alcoholic ingredient in eggnog recipes. However, due to disruptions in global trade during the American Revolutionary War period, rum became increasingly scarce and difficult to acquire. As a result, rum was often substituted with homemade whiskey or "moonshine" produced locally by independent distillers across the new United States.

This shift from rum to moonshine in eggnog may help explain how the drink eventually became so strongly associated with Christmas celebrations in the States. As the story goes, the native spirit was a practical winter warmer during the cold holiday season when expensive imported rum was not as readily available.

The moonshine offered both the desired alcoholic potency and welcomed heat for those gathering with family and friends.

Over time, the tradition of enjoying this boozy beverage around Christmas endured and became ingrained in American folklore and seasonal traditions.

While rum regained popularity after the war, moonshine eggnog had already taken hold as a favored Christmas custom that still resonates today.

The Eggnog effect – a funny fictitious story. It was Christmas Eve when everything that could go wrong, did go wrong, in the most hilarious way possible. It all started with Uncle Bob. Uncle Bob was known in the family for his "legendary" eggnog.

The problem was, Uncle Bob's eggnog was more "nog" so to speak, than egg, if you catch my drift. This year, he decided to make a double batch.

By 7 PM, the entire family, from Grandma Betty to little cousin Timmy, was feeling rather "festive." Aunt Linda, who never touched alcohol, was giggling uncontrollably at the Christmas tree, convinced it was winking at her.

Grandpa Joe had turned into an amateur stand-up comedian, delivering punchlines that only he found funny. The rest of the family, in their eggnog-induced haze, laughed along anyway.

Outside, a blizzard had started, piling snow higher and higher. By 8 PM, the snow had reached the windowsills, and Uncle Bob, in his infinite wisdom, declared it the perfect opportunity for a snowball fight. The family, fueled by eggnog and holiday spirit, bundled up and took the party outside.

The Snowball Fiasco. What started as a friendly snowball fight quickly erupted into an all-out snowball war. Cousin Jenny, an aspiring softball player, had a cannon for an arm and was merciless.

Uncle Bob, ever the instigator, crafted an enormous snowball that he could barely lift. When he tried to throw it, he lost his balance, and the gigantic snowball landed on him, knocking him over like a cartoon character. Everyone roared with laughter.

Grandma Betty's Snowman. Meanwhile, Grandma Betty, who had also indulged in the eggnog, decided to make a snowman. She worked diligently, but her snowman had a rather unusual shape—a head where the belly should be and vice versa. She proudly named it "Snowmando."

The Big Finish. Just when they thought the night couldn't get any funnier, the family dog, Max, got loose and started chasing everyone. People were slipping, sliding, and falling into the snow, laughing so hard they could barely stand up. Aunt Linda tried to climb a snowbank to escape Max, only to tumble down the other side, landing in a heap of giggles.

Finally, exhausted and freezing, the family retreated inside. They gathered around the fire, drying off and recounting the night's events.

Uncle Bob, now sporting a large snowball-sized bruise, raised his cup of eggnog for a toast. "To the best Christmas ever," he said, and everyone cheered.

That Christmas Eve, amid the drunken antics, too much snow, and unexpected hilarity, the family discovered that sometimes the best memories are made when things don't go according to plan, and turned out to be one of the funniest Christmas events they ever had.

The Misplaced Ornament Game.

What You'll Need: A collection of unusual ornaments (like mini rubber chickens, tiny fake food items, or miniature garden gnomes), a camera, or a smartphone.

The Game: Secretly replace a few regular ornaments on the Christmas tree with the unusual ones. Make sure they are well-hidden among the branches.

Then, create a festive scavenger hunt where family and friends have to find these odd ornaments. Capture their reactions as they locate each bizarre item. To add an extra layer of hilarity, you can offer a silly prize for the person who finds the most unusual ornaments.

The Chaotic Thompson Household. This is a fictional story. It was the morning of December 24th, and the Thompson household was a whirlwind of Christmas chaos. With just one day until the big celebration, every family member was bustling around, trying to get everything ready for their annual Christmas Eve party.

The Gift Wrap Fiasco. Mom was in the living room, surrounded by a mountain of gifts and a dwindling supply of wrapping paper. She had somehow managed to cut every piece just a bit too small for the gifts they were meant to cover.

After futile attempts to stretch and tape the paper into place, she decided to go with a creative approach. Soon, the gifts were wrapped in layers of mismatched paper, newspaper, and even a few pages from Dad's crossword puzzle book.

The result was a colorful collage of Christmas cheer that had the family in stitches.

The Kitchen Commotion. Meanwhile, Dad was in the kitchen attempting to bake his famous Christmas cookies. In his haste, he grabbed the salt instead of sugar, creating a batch that had everyone puckering their lips in surprise.

In an attempt to salvage the situation, he declared them "savory cookies" and paired them with cheese and crackers. The family couldn't stop laughing at his culinary creativity, and the cookies became an unexpected hit.

The Tree Topper Trouble. In the den, the kids were tasked with decorating the Christmas tree. As they reached for the star to place on top, they realized that last year's mishap had left it bent and wobbly.

Not to be deterred, they fashioned a new tree topper out of an old Santa hat stuffed with cotton balls. When placed atop the tree, it gave the impression of Santa peeking over the branches, much to everyone's delight.

The Pet Predicament. As if things weren't hectic enough, the family's dog, Max, and cat, Whiskers, decided to join in the chaos.

Max, in his excitement, found the leftover wrapping paper and began to shred it into confetti, while Whiskers, determined not to be outdone, climbed into the tree, causing it to sway precariously.

The family rushed to rescue both pets, which resulted in a tangle of lights, laughter, and love.

Last-Minute Guest List. Just when they thought things were under control, Aunt Edna called to say she was bringing a few "surprise guests" to the party.

The family scrambled to set extra places at the table, using everything from folding chairs to the piano bench.

When Aunt Edna arrived with her guests—three of her friends from her knitting club—the Thompsons welcomed them with open arms, grateful for the extra company and stories of knitting adventures.

The Party's Unexpected Hit. As the evening wore on and the party began, the mismatched decorations, unusual cookies, and impromptu seating arrangements became the talk of the gathering.

The guests praised the Thompsons for their creativity and ability to embrace the chaos with humor and grace.

By the end of the night, everyone agreed it was the most memorable Christmas Eve party they had ever attended.

In the end, the Great Christmas Chaos of the Thompson Household became a cherished family legend, reminding them each year that the true magic of Christmas lies not in perfection but in the joy, laughter, and love shared with family and friends.

Atheist.

"I once wanted to become an atheist, but I gave up - they have no holidays." – **Henny Youngman**

Twas the Night Before Christmas.

While Clement Clarke Moore's iconic 1823 holiday poem is popularly known for its memorable opening line "'Twas the Night Before Christmas," the work's actual title is "A Visit from St. Nicholas."

This classic verse has become ingrained in Western culture as a hallmark of Christmas tradition, its familiar first line serving as shorthand for the joyful narrative within.

However, for accuracy's sake, it is worth noting that "A Visit from St. Nicholas" is the poem's formal name according to its original publication, with "'Twas the Night Before Christmas" representing more of a colloquialism that has persisted in popular parlance.

Both titles remain fitting for Moore's festive work that recounts St. Nicholas's Christmas Eve journey. Regardless of what it is called, the poem continues to be a cherished part of the seasonal celebrations of many.

Clement Clark Moore (July 15, 1779 – July 10, 1863)

Why do we celebrate Christmas in December?

When was Jesus born? The Bible doesn't specify the day Jesus was born. As we all know, the celebration of Christmas is a significant religious festival that marks the birth of Jesus Christ.

Most annually observe this commemoration on December 25th, as the Roman Catholic Church designated this date to honor the nativity of Jesus.

The actual birth date of Jesus is unknown and remains uncertain. Based on historical biblical accounts, most scholars estimate that Jesus was born between 6 BC to 4 BC, as the Roman Catholic decision to celebrate Christmas on December

25th was partly made to co-opt pagan solstice festivals held on or around that date, but the exact reason seems unclear.

In any event, Christmas has evolved beyond its specifically religious origins to take on broader secular cultural significance in many societies. For many people around the world, it provides an annual festival of gift-giving, social gatherings with family and friends, feasting, music, dancing, and other merriments to celebrate light and community during the darkest time of the year in the Northern Hemisphere. As such, Christmas today represents both a commemoration of the foundational event in Christianity as well as broader winter celebrations.

Few know there are Christians who celebrate Christmas on a different day other than the usual December 25th. In countries with sizable Orthodox Christian populations, such as Russia, Ukraine, and Romania, the religious holiday of Christmas is observed on January 7th. This is due to the Orthodox Churches continuing to follow the Julian calendar, rather than adopting the Gregorian calendar used by their Western Christian counterparts.

Similarly, some Greek Orthodox Christians commemorate the Nativity of Christ and associated festivities on January 7th as well.

The Story of Rudolf.

While Rudolph became a beloved Christmas character, his origins were based more on commercial promotion than creative inspiration.

The story of Rudolph first emerged in 1939 not as a standalone work but as a marketing tool. Specifically, Rudolph was conceived as a means to drive sales for the Montgomery Ward department store during the holiday season.

Robert L. May devised the Rudolph concept did so with the intent of including a coloring book featuring the character in Montgomery Ward's Christmas catalog, which was distributed to millions of customers. An advertising professional strategically designed Rudolph to boost store traffic and revenues.

The tale took on a life of its own through the marketing efforts. Rudolf's very first appearance was in a free giveaway meant to promote purchases from Montgomery Ward during Christmas, not as a standalone work intended as entertainment or education. Rudolph's marketing origins, though rarely acknowledged today, played a key role in bringing the character to widespread popularity.

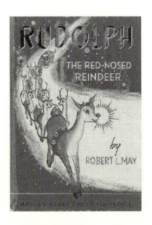

A Robert L. May book

Christmas Curiosities by Bruce Miller

Oddities at Christmas Time Around the World.

Christmas is a time of joy, and celebration, and sometimes very funny things occur around the age-old traditions.

While many of us are familiar with the standard practices of decorating trees, exchanging gifts, and singing carols, some places take their holiday cheer to a whole new level of hilarity.

Here are some laugh-out-loud funny and extreme oddities that make Christmas time in the USA, UK, Canada, Australia, and other countries truly unforgettable.

USA: The Great Christmas Lights Fight. In the USA, Christmas light displays can get pretty competitive, but nothing beats the annual "Great Christmas Lights Fight" in a small town in Texas.

The Johnson family, who have won the competition three years in a row, decided to up their game. They created a synchronized light show with over 100,000 lights, all set to dubstep versions of Christmas carols. The display was so intense that it caused a minor traffic jam, and a few drivers even reported getting "Christmas light-induced headaches."

But the real kicker was their giant inflatable Santa Claus, which somehow got loose and floated down Main Street, causing chaos and laughter as people chased after it.

Local news dubbed it the "Santa Runaway" incident, and it's become a legendary story in the town's Christmas lore.

UK: The Pantomime Pandemonium. In the UK, Christmas pantomimes are a beloved tradition, but sometimes they go hilariously awry.

One year, a small theater troupe in Birmingham decided to put on a pantomime of "Jack and the Beanstalk." Things got off to a rocky start when the actor playing the giant got stuck in his oversized costume and had to be wheeled off stage in a shopping cart.

The real hilarity ensued during the famous "he's behind you" scene, where a mischievous audience member decided to dress up as a cow and sneak onto the stage. The actors caught off guard, and couldn't keep a straight face, and the audience roared with laughter.

The cow, now a local celebrity, even got a mention in the town's Christmas parade.

Canada: The Polar Bear Plunge Prank. In Canada, the Polar Bear Plunge is a popular winter tradition. Have you ever wondered what it would be like to jump into icy waters? Would you be brave enough to do it to raise money for charity?

In Vancouver, a group of pranksters decided to take this to the next level. They dressed up as penguins and pretended to be part of a "Penguin Plunge."

When they jumped into the frigid water, they started squawking and flapping their wings, much to the bewilderment of onlookers. The sight of grown adults waddling around in penguin suits and diving into icy waters had everyone in stitches.

The prank went viral, and the "Penguin Plunge" has since become an annual tradition, raising even more money for charity.

Australia: The Kangaroo Christmas Caper. Christmas in Australia is a sunny affair, but that doesn't mean it's without its oddities. One year, in a small town in Queensland, a group of locals decided to dress up kangaroos in Santa hats and reindeer antlers. The kangaroos, surprisingly cooperative, hopped around town spreading Christmas cheer.

However, things took a turn for the absurd when one particularly enthusiastic kangaroo, dubbed "Roo-dolph," decided to crash a local Christmas barbecue. He hopped right up to the grill, snatched a sausage, and bounded away, leaving everyone in fits of laughter. The town now has a "Roo-dolph" float in their Christmas parade, complete with a giant sausage.

Germany: The Krampus Karaoke. In Germany, the Christmas season is marked by the terrifying figure of Krampus, who punishes naughty children. One festive season, a group of friends in Munich decided to host a "Krampus Karaoke" night at their local pub. Participants had to sing Christmas carols while dressed as Krampus, complete with chains, bells, and scary masks.

The sight of people belting out "Silent Night" and "Jingle Bells" while looking like demonic creatures was both hilarious and unsettling.

Rockefeller Center's Christmas Tree Tradition.

The Rockefeller Center Christmas tree tradition began quite modestly in 1931. With construction underway on what would become one of New York City's most famous landmarks, workers erected a small, unadorned evergreen tree at the construction site.

This served as a simple acknowledgment of the Christmas season and as a symbol of hope during the tough economic times of the Great Depression era.

In the nearly ninety years since the Rockefeller Center Christmas tree has evolved into one of the most famous and spectacular holiday centerpieces in the world.

Today's towering trees, some reaching heights over one hundred feet, are quite different from that first small tree. They are festooned with over 50,000 multi-colored LED lights, totaling nearly five miles of illumination.

Live high-definition broadcasts from Rockefeller Center reach millions worldwide each holiday season to highlight this Grande dame of Christmas trees in all her illuminated glory.

From its humble beginnings to its current iconic status, the Rockefeller Center Christmas tree tradition has grown exponentially while retaining its role in celebrating the holidays in New York City and around the globe.

Rockefeller Center Christmas Tree

Memorable Celebrity Christmas Stories.

The holiday season brings out the best and sometimes the quirkiest in people, and celebrities are no exception. From movie stars and TV personalities to sports icons and musicians, many well-known figures have found unique and entertaining ways to celebrate Christmas.

Here are some true stories of odd and little-known things celebrities have done during the holiday season.

George Clooney's Elaborate Gift Prank. George Clooney is known for his sense of humor and love for pranks, and one Christmas, he took his shenanigans to a whole new level. George, who has a penchant for elaborate jokes, decided to surprise his close friends with a truly unforgettable gift. He gave fourteen of his dearest friends one million dollars each in cash in a suitcase.

The story goes that Clooney invited his friends over for dinner and handed them the suitcases, telling them he wanted to give back to those who had supported him throughout his career. To make it even more memorable, he reportedly hired a van with "Gifts Galore" emblazoned on the side to deliver the suitcases.

While this act of generosity might not be considered odd in itself, the sheer scale and surprise element certainly make it an incredible Christmas story.

Martha Stewart's Glitter Bombs. Martha Stewart, the queen of domesticity, is known for her impeccable taste and elaborate holiday decorations.

However, one Christmas, she decided to mix things up with a bit of mischief. Stewart created "glitter bombs" as part of her holiday gift-giving. These were beautifully wrapped packages that, when opened, exploded with a burst of glitter.

Stewart sent these glitter bombs to several of her friends and colleagues, including some high-profile celebrities. The recipients were reportedly both amused and exasperated as they found themselves covered in glitter, which, as everyone knows, is notoriously difficult to clean up.

Martha Stewart's playful prank added a touch of sparkle—and chaos—to the holiday season.

David Beckham's Christmas Tree Challenge. David Beckham, the iconic soccer star, is known for his competitive spirit, and one Christmas, he turned his festive decorations into a challenge. Beckham decided to see who could create the most extravagant Christmas tree in his household. The competition included his wife, Victoria Beckham, and their four children.

David went all out, enlisting the help of professional decorators to adorn his tree with thousands of lights, custom ornaments, and even a mini soccer pitch at the base.

Victoria, not to be outdone, created a chic, minimalist tree with designer decorations.

The children each had their own unique takes, from a superhero-themed tree to one covered in homemade ornaments.

The Beckham family's Christmas tree challenge became a beloved tradition, highlighting their creativity and playful rivalry.

Ellen DeGeneres's 12 Days of Giveaways. Ellen DeGeneres is well-known for her surprising generosity, especially during the holiday season. She hosted the "12 Days of Giveaways" on her show, where audience members receive an array of extravagant gifts.

However, one year DeGeneres decided to take her holiday spirit to the next level by surprising unsuspecting people outside of the studio.

DeGeneres and her team visited hospitals, schools, and even random homes, spreading holiday cheer with surprise gifts. In one memorable instance, she showed up at a small, struggling toy store and bought out their entire inventory, which she then donated to local children's charities.

DeGeneres's spontaneous acts of kindness brought joy to countless people, making for an unforgettable Christmas season.

Snoop Dogg's Christmas Album. Snoop Dogg, the legendary rapper, is full of surprises, and one of his most unexpected ventures was releasing a Christmas album. In 2008, Snoop Dogg released "Snoop Dogg Presents Christmas in tha Dogg House," a holiday album featuring a mix of traditional Christmas carols and original tracks with a distinctive hip-hop twist.

The album includes quirky tracks like "Xmas on Soul Train" and "A Pimp's Christmas Song," blending Snoop's signature style with holiday cheer. The album's release was accompanied by a series of humorous music videos featuring Snoop dressed as Santa Claus, complete with a fur-trimmed coat and oversized sunglasses.

Snoop Dogg's Christmas album added a unique and entertaining twist to the holiday music scene.

Mariah Carey's Annual Christmas Concert: "All I Want for Christmas Is You: A Night of Joy and Festivity" From 2014 through 2019, Mariah Carey with her five-octave vocal range performed her iconic hit "All I Want for Christmas Is You" a timeless Christmas anthem, and held an annual Christmas concert series which began in 2014.

The concert series has been held in various cities around the world, including New York City, London, and Paris. Each year, the show featured classic Christmas songs, dazzling performances, and a touch of Mariah's signature glamour.

"All I Want for Christmas Is You: A Night of Joy and Festivity" is more than just a concert—it's a full-fledged holiday extravaganza. The stage is transformed into a winter wonderland, complete with twinkling lights, snow-covered trees, and elaborate decorations that evoke the spirit of the season. Mariah Carey herself is often adorned in stunning, glittering outfits that add to the festive atmosphere.

The setlist for the concert includes a mix of Mariah's beloved holiday hits, such as "Santa Claus Is Coming to Town," "O Holy Night," and, of course, "All I Want for Christmas Is You."

In addition to her Christmas classics, Mariah also performs some of her other chart-topping songs, ensuring that there's something for everyone to enjoy.

The show is known for its high-energy performances and elaborate choreography, featuring a talented ensemble of dancers and musicians. Special guest appearances by other artists and celebrities often add an extra layer of excitement to the event.

One of the unique aspects of Mariah Carey's Christmas concert series is the sense of community and togetherness it fosters. Fans from all walks of life come together to share in the joy of the holiday season, united by their love for Mariah's music. The concert is an opportunity for people to create lasting memories with family and friends, making it a cherished tradition for many.

Mariah Carey herself often interacts with the audience, sharing personal anecdotes and expressing her gratitude for their support. Her genuine warmth and enthusiasm for the holiday season shine through, creating an intimate and heartfelt connection with her fans.

In addition to spreading holiday cheer, the concert series has also had a positive impact on charitable causes. Mariah Carey has used the platform to support various organizations, encouraging concertgoers to give back to their communities during the season of giving.

Mariah Carey created a magical experience that brought joy and festivity to audiences worldwide. As the concert series continues to grow in popularity, it remains a testament to the enduring power of holiday music and the spirit of togetherness that defines the season.

Taylor Swift: The Year She Became Santa Swift. It was the Christmas season of 2014, and Taylor Swift was riding high on the success of her latest album, "1989." Despite her busy schedule, Taylor was determined to spread some holiday cheer in a unique and memorable way. Little did her fans know, she had a special surprise up her sleeve that would touch hearts and create unforgettable memories.

Taylor, known for her deep connection with her fans, had been secretly following some of their stories through social media. She wanted to give back to the people who had supported her so fervently, and what better time to do it than during the season of giving? So, she decided to become "Santa Swift."

With the help of her team, Taylor meticulously selected a few fans who had shared their personal struggles and triumphs online. She spent hours reading their stories, getting to know their personalities, and understanding what would bring them joy. Then, she went to work, personalizing gifts and writing heartfelt letters.

So, on a chilly December evening, Taylor donned a festive Santa hat and set out to deliver her presents. She visited the homes of several fans, each time leaving them completely astonished and overjoyed.

One of the most heartwarming visits was to a young fan named Rebecca, who had been going through a tough time due to her parents' recent divorce.

Rebecca was an ardent "Swiftie" and had often turned to Taylor's music for comfort. On that particular evening, Rebecca was sitting in her living room, listening to "Shake It Off" and trying to get into the Christmas spirit. Suddenly, there was a knock on the door. Her mother opened it to find none other than Taylor Swift standing there, holding a large, beautifully wrapped gift.

Rebecca's jaw dropped, and she couldn't believe her eyes. Taylor walked in with a warm smile and hugged Rebecca tightly. They sat down together, and Taylor handed her the gift. Inside was a custom-made guitar with Rebecca's name engraved on it, along with a handwritten note from Taylor, encouraging her to pursue her dreams and keep her head high no matter what life threw at her.

The two spent the evening chatting, laughing, and even singing a few songs together. Taylor's genuine warmth and kindness left a lasting impact on Rebecca and her family. For that night, the living room wasn't just a place in their house—it was transformed into a magical space filled with love, music, and the true spirit of Christmas.

Taylor's impromptu visits didn't stop there. She continued to surprise fans, each time bringing her infectious joy and heartfelt gifts. The stories quickly spread across social media, with fans sharing their incredible experiences and expressing their gratitude.

That Christmas, Taylor Swift didn't just give out material gifts; she gave her time, her presence, and her genuine care. She showed that even a global superstar could take the time to make a personal connection and touch the hearts of those who needed it most.

And so, the legend of "Santa Swift" was born—a story of a superstar who used her fame and resources to bring warmth, joy, and a little bit of Christmas magic into the lives of her fans.

The Essence of Christmas. The true spirit of Christmas is all about giving with an open heart, and expecting nothing in return. It's a season where our happiness blossoms from the joy we see in others' smiles. Christmas embodies the beauty of selflessness, encouraging us to dedicate our time and energy to those around us. During this magical time, we let go of trivial worries and focus on what truly matters—love, kindness, and togetherness.

-- Thomas S. Monson

Did you know? In Iceland, there exists a Christmas tradition where books are gifted on Christmas Eve and the recipients spend the night engaged in reading activities. This cultural practice is referred to as "Jolabokaflod," loosely translated to "Christmas Book Flood."

In 2014, Thrissur, India was home to the largest assemblage of individuals dressed as Santa Claus, totaling 18,112 people who congregated to set a world record.

Invented in 1847 in London by Tom Smith, Australia was the birthplace of the world's largest Christmas cracker in 1991. It measured over 207 feet in length and 13 feet in diameter. [19]

In 1966, the Arizona Department of Public Safety accommodated the wish of a young boy named Chris Greicius, who was battling leukemia, to experience life as a police officer. This touching event paved the way for the formation of the Make-A-Wish Foundation, a global non-profit dedicated to fulfilling the wishes of critically ill children.

In 2015, the town of Washington, Illinois played host to a heartwarming experience involving a young boy named Dax Locke battling a rare form of leukemia. In an act of compassion and solidarity, the community banded together to facilitate an early Christmas celebration in September to allow Dax the opportunity to engage in holiday festivities before his passing. This gesture brought immense joy to Dax and his family during their final moments together and created lasting memories.

The Christmas Miracle of the Halifax Explosion.

In the early morning hours of December 6, 1917, the bustling port city of Halifax, Nova Scotia, was teeming with activity. The First World War was in full swing, and Halifax served as a critical hub for transporting troops and supplies across the Atlantic.

That morning, an unfortunate series of events led to one of the largest man-made explosions before the atomic age, forever changing the course of many lives but also paving the way for a heartwarming Christmas tale that few people know about.

The Norwegian vessel, SS Imo, and the French cargo ship SS Mont-Blanc collided in the Narrows, a strait connecting the upper Halifax Harbor to Bedford Basin. The Mont-Blanc, loaded with explosives, caught fire and ignited, causing a cataclysmic explosion that devastated the city. Thousands were injured, nearly 2,000 lost their lives, and countless homes were destroyed. It was a tragedy of unimaginable scale at that time.

The Halifax Explosion

Amidst the chaos, the people of Halifax were in dire need of immediate help. News of the disaster quickly spread, and one of the first to respond was the city of Boston, Massachusetts.

Boston organized a massive relief effort within hours, sending a train loaded with medical supplies, food, and volunteers to aid the stricken city. The Boston Red Cross and other organizations worked tirelessly to provide support, and their efforts were instrumental in the recovery process.

As Christmas approached, the spirit of giving and compassion was more evident than ever. The people of Halifax, grateful for the swift and generous response from Boston, wanted to express their heartfelt thanks. Despite their losses and hardships, they decided to send a special gift to their friends in Boston. [20]

In December 1917, Halifax sent a majestic 46-foot Christmas tree to Boston showing their gratitude for the city's extraordinary assistance. This gesture of goodwill not only brightened the holidays but also forged a lasting bond between the two cities. The tree, a symbol of resilience and camaraderie, was placed in Boston Common, where it brought joy and hope to all who saw it.

The tradition of sending a Christmas tree from Halifax to Boston has continued every year since 1971 when the practice was officially revived. Each year, a carefully selected tree is cut down and transported to Boston, where it is lit in a festive ceremony that marks the beginning of the holiday season. The tree serves as a reminder of the enduring friendship between the two cities and the power of compassion and community in the face of adversity.

This Christmas tree tradition between Halifax and Boston is more than just a piece of trivia; it is a testament to the human spirit's capacity for kindness and gratitude. The story of the Halifax Explosion and the subsequent Christmas tree gift is a poignant reminder that even in the darkest times, acts of generosity and goodwill can light the way for a brighter future.

This heartwarming tale not only celebrates the true essence of Christmas but also highlights the importance of coming together in times of need. It's a story that encourages us all to remember the power of empathy, the joy of giving, and the bonds that connect us, no matter how far apart we may be.

So, as you enjoy the festive season, take a moment to reflect on this story of resilience and unity. Let it inspire you to spread a little more kindness and cheer, and to appreciate the hidden wonders and connections that make the holiday season truly magical!

The Deeper Meaning of Christmas. The Spirit of Christmas is a time for generosity, community, reflection, renewal, compassion, and celebrating humanity. It encourages generosity through thoughtful gifts and kind acts without expectation of reciprocation. It brings people together to reconnect with family and friends, strengthen community bonds, and mend relationships.

The season fosters reflection on both the positive and negative of the past year with gratitude for life's blessings. It symbolizes hope for a new beginning and renewal even in challenging times. Christmas calls for compassion towards those facing hardships and extending help to those in need.

At its core, Christmas celebrates the human spirit with themes of humility, peace, and innate human goodness. Traditions create intergenerational memories that preserve cultural heritage.

Despite busy preparations, Christmas' true essence lies in finding inner peace, pausing for reflection, and a sense of calm and contentment. Stripping away from commercial aspects, the holiday centers on human connection and bettering society through its intangible values of love, generosity and togetherness.

Final thought. By sharing the story of Christmas and the things and events that happen, and by sharing smiles, singing songs, catching up with friends, embodying its spirit, and sharing love, it becomes truly possible to spread joy, happiness, and peace worldwide. Enjoy the season and keep this wonderful spirit all year!

We hope you enjoyed the book!

Thank you for reading! If you liked the book, we sincerely appreciate your taking a few moments to leave a review.

Thank you again very much!

Merry Christmas and Happy New Year to you and yours!

Sincerely,

Bruce Miller

About the author.

Bruce Miller. Bruce Miller is an award-winning author. As an attorney and businessman, he has achieved success in multiple career paths. However, Mr. Miller's passion lies in continuous learning and sharing knowledge. He spends his days studying, writing, and exploring the ever-changing world around us.

Mr. Miller has written over 60 books in various genres. Several of his works have become bestsellers. In addition to his literary works, Mr. Miller is also an aviator and active member of several professional organizations related to his interests.

We Want to Hear from You!

"There usually is a way to do things better and there is opportunity when you find it." - Thomas Edison

We love to hear your thoughts and suggestions on anything and please feel free to contact me at bruce@teamgolfwell.com

Other Books by Bruce Miller

Beware the Ides of March: A Novel Based on Psychic Readings (Awarded Distinguished Favorite by the NYC Big Book Award 2023).

Dragonflies: A Novel About What Men Think of Women (Awarded Distinguished Favorite by the NYC Big Book Award 2024).

The Book of Unusual Sports Knowledge.

Guy Wilson Creating Golf Excellence: The Genesis of Lydia Ko & More Stars.

For a Great Fisherman Who Has Everything: A Funny Book for Fishermen.

For the Golfer Who Has Everything: A Funny Golf Book.

The Funniest Quotations to Brighten Every Day: Brilliant, Inspiring, and Hilarious Thoughts from Great Minds.

For a Tennis Player Who Has Everything: A Funny Tennis Book, and many more...

References

[1] The Christmas Truce, Wikipedia, https://en.wikipedia.org/wiki/Christmas_truce.
[2] https://kids.guinnessworldrecords.com/news/2022/12/6-of-the-best-christmas-records-ever-729635
[3] Ibid.
[4] Bethel, Maine's World's Tallest SnowWoman, YouTube, https://www.youtube.com/watch?v=VrZs2EAccOU
[5] By Chris Darling - originally posted to Flickr as 95% had their cameras trained on CC BY 2.0, https://commons.wikimedia.org/w/index.php?curid=6244964
[6] Longest Chain of sleds – Guinness World Record, YouTube, https://www.youtube.com/watch?v=QHZmlxq_zQU&t=8s
[7] Ibid. s
[8] https://www.guinnessworldrecords.com/world-records/most-lights-on-a-residential-property
[9] Good Morning America, YouTube, https://www.youtube.com/watch?v=w-4KJv2wDaY&t=12s
[10] World's Largest Floating Christmas Tree, Guinness World Records, https://www.guinnessworldrecords.com/world-records/largest-floating-christmas-tree
[11] Guinness World Records, Best selling single for Christmas, https://www.guinnessworldrecords.com/world-records/72375-best-selling-single-for-christmas
[12] White House Christmas Tree, Wikipedia, https://en.wikipedia.org/wiki/White_House_Christmas_tree
[13] Ibid.
[14] NRF Says Census Data Shows 2023 Holiday Sales Grew 3.8% to Record $964.4 Billion, National Retail Federation,

https://nrf.com/media-center/press-releases/nrf-says-census-data-shows-2023-holiday-sales-grew-38-record-9644#
[15] Candy Canes, Wikipedia, https://en.wikipedia.org/wiki/Candy_cane
[16] Ibid.
[17] Xmas, Wikipedia, https://en.wikipedia.org/wiki/Xmas
[18] Icelandic Christmas Folklore, Wikipedia, https://en.wikipedia.org/wiki/Icelandic_Christmas_folklore
[19] Christmas cracker, Wikipedia, https://en.wikipedia.org/wiki/Christmas_cracker
[20] Boston- Halifax Relations, Wikipedia, https://en.wikipedia.org/wiki/Boston%E2%80%93Halifax_relations

Made in the USA
Middletown, DE
16 December 2024